Shaping the New Europe

CHATHAM HOUSE PAPERS

A European Programme Publication
Programme Director: Susie Symes

The Royal Institute of International Affairs, at Chatham House in London, has provided an impartial forum for discussion and debate on current international issues for some 70 years. Its resident research fellows, specialized information resources, and range of publications, conferences, and meetings span the fields of international politics, economics, and security. The Institute is independent of government.

Chatham House Papers are short monographs on current policy problems which have been commissioned by the RIIA. In preparing the papers, authors are advised by a study group of experts convened by the RIIA, and publication of a paper indicates that the Institute regards it as an authoritative contribution to the public debate. The Institute does not, however, hold opinions of its own; the views expressed in this publication are the responsibility of the author.

CHATHAM HOUSE PAPERS

Shaping the New Europe

Hugh Miall

The Royal Institute of International Affairs

Pinter Publishers
London

Pinter Publishers Limited
25 Floral Street, Covent Garden, London WC2E 9DS, United Kingdom

First published in 1993

© Royal Institute of International Affairs, 1993

British Library Cataloguing in Publication Data
A CIP catalogue record for this book is available from the British Library

ISBN 1-85567- 020-4 (Paperback)
  1-85567-119-0 (Hardback)

1001178329

Typeset by Koinonia Limited
Printed and bound in Great Britain by
Biddles Limited, Guildford and King's Lynn

CONTENTS

ACKNOWLEDGMENTS

This paper is the product of a project entitled 'Changing Paradigms of European Order', carried out by the European Programme at the Royal Institute of International Affairs. It aims to interpret how long-term trends in western and eastern Europe have shaped the post-Cold War order. To fit this large subject into a short space, this study concentrates on trends in governance, economics and international relations. The post-Cold War order continues to change at a rapid pace and its ultimate shape remains uncertain; nevertheless, it is rewarding to write about it as it evolves, for the patterns taking shape since 1989 seem likely to influence events for many years to come.

The National Institute for Research Advancement, Tokyo, generously provided financial support for this project. I thank them for this and for their encouragement. I am grateful to the participants in the project's steering committee and study groups for their contributions and insights. I also thank the policy-makers and academics who gave their time during my visits to central and eastern Europe. I am especially indebted to those who commented on earlier drafts and to present and former colleagues in the European Programme for their guidance, help and criticisms, in particular Helen Wallace, former director of the Programme. I also wish to thank the librarians at Chatham House, the members of the Publications Department and the many others in the House whose support has contributed to this project. Of course I am responsible for the accuracy of the text and the views it expresses.

August 1993   Hugh Miall

Europe after the First World War

Europe in 1993

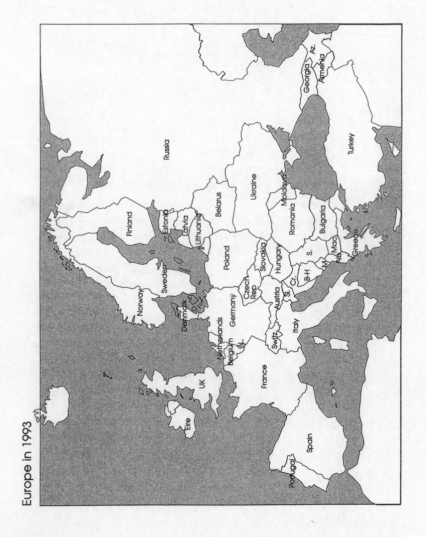

1

PAST EUROPEAN ORDERS: FROM THE CONGRESS OF VIENNA TO THE CSCE

Introduction

In early 1989 the postwar order in Europe was still largely intact. The continent was divided, politically and economically, along lines set by the end of the Second World War and confirmed at the Yalta and Potsdam conferences. To the west, states with multi-party democracies participated in the global market economy. To the east, communist regimes dominated politics, and economies were subject to a system of central planning organized in the interests of the Soviet bloc. Along the dividing line, running between the German states, seven million troops confronted each other, armed with conventional and nuclear weapons.

Three years later, the political order in Europe was transformed. In June 1989 a non-communist government took power in Poland. The Soviet Union did not attempt to intervene. On 9 November 1989 the East German government, under pressure from the stream of departing citizens, breached the Berlin Wall. By December 1989 democratic revolutions had overthrown the communist regimes in Czechoslovakia, Hungary and Bulgaria. In October 1990 Germany was unified. In December 1991 the Soviet Union was dismantled.

With the break-up of Comecon and the Warsaw Pact, Europe was no longer divided into rival blocs. Military tensions, already fading by 1989, ebbed away. In 1990 member states of NATO and the Warsaw Pact declared that they were no longer adversaries. The unification of Germany created a state which straddles the old East–West divide. The new democracies in eastern Europe are seeking to forge economic and political ties with the West, and west European states are responding.

These remarkable changes have created a new order in Europe. Is it

1

possible that Europe might, as suggested by the 1990 Charter of Paris of the Conference on Security and Cooperation in Europe (CSCE), escape 'the legacy of its past', and create an effective framework for security and cooperation? Does the prospect of enlargement of the European Community create a vehicle through which the peoples of Europe can achieve 'ever closer union'? Do the political will and the necessary historical conditions exist for the development of a political and economic community throughout the wider Europe?

Two opposite processes appeared to be under way in different halves of the continent. In the west, the process of integration, driven initially by economic forces, acquired political momentum after 1989. The member states of the EC were already pooling elements of state sovereignty and implementing Community legislation into national law. The Single European Market, and the plan to extend it to include the countries of the European Free Trade Association (EFTA), promised to create a market of 370 million people, with free flow of people, goods, services and capital. The proposal to create a European Union was a further step towards closer integration. In the east, by contrast, the disintegration of the old political and economic system was still working itself out. The east central European governments were quick to cut their ties with the former Soviet Union, although it would take longer to reform their economic systems. In the Balkans, the fall of communist regimes fanned into flame old ethnic and national conflicts, leading to civil war in Yugoslavia. In the former Soviet Union, the collapse of the centre led to plunging economic output, accompanied by struggles for power within and between the successor states.

What is the shape of the new Europe which will follow these upheavals? The political map has changed, and may change again. In some respects, the new pattern resembles that of Europe after the First World War. Russia is in reduced circumstances, Germany is large and centrally placed, and there is a swathe of weak independent states in eastern and central Europe. In other respects, the pattern is entirely new, especially if we think about Europe from other perspectives. How appropriate is it, in 1992, still to see the European map in terms of national borders? If the EC is considered a political unit, its growth seems set to continue, from the six in 1952, to the nine in 1973, to ten in 1981 and twelve in 1986, perhaps to twenty or more if the EFTA and east central European countries join.

If we look at Europe in terms of cross-national transactions, movements of people, cultural links and economic flows, western Europe has a much richer network internally than it has with eastern Europe, and is linked more tightly to the United States and to other OECD countries than to eastern Europe. West European states manage their affairs far more through globally based groupings – such as OECD, the Group of Seven (G-7), G-24, the General Agreement on Tariffs and Trade (GATT) – than through ones in which the east Europeans participate. To the extent that functional relationships and transactions drive the process of political integration, western Europe can be expected to integrate more strongly with other partners in the world economy than with the new market economies in eastern Europe.

Another way of looking at Europe is in terms of economic structures. The triad of the USA, EC-12 and Japan already had a dominant place at the core of the world order before 1989, with newly industrialized countries in the semi-periphery and less developed countries in the periphery. The collapse of the bipolar system has thrown this pattern into sharper relief. There is also a core–periphery pattern within Europe. In western Europe, it is the major cities and industrial regions such as the Rhine valley and northern Italy which drive the pace of socioeconomic change. Around them is a semi-periphery of less developed regions and industrial areas. As eastern Europe enters the economic system of the West, its relatively unmodernized societies, with their low living standards, will be drawn in as a new part of the periphery.

There is no doubt that the events of 1989–91 mark a major change within the international system. The bipolar system has come to an end and multipolarity has replaced it. The collapse of the Soviet Union has left the United States as the sole superpower, though the economic position of the United States is in relative decline. International alignments have changed not only in central Europe, the Baltics and the Balkans but also in the Middle East, Asia and other parts of the world.

A more fundamental question is whether events in Europe indicate that the international system itself has changed. Trends towards a global economy and global communications appear to be driving the world beyond an order based on the nation-state. States already manage their affairs increasingly through collective organizations and regimes. In western Europe, an area traditionally rich in national cultures, the process of integration is furthest advanced. If continued, this pattern of development may have important implications for the international system as a whole.

A related change in the European state system is the general acceptance of the disutility of war in relations between major powers. The process of detente and the ending of the Cold War were accompanied by the development of a new security regime in Europe, in which the military forces of the former blocs began to exchange information and cooperate to a remarkable degree. The break-up of the Soviet Union and Yugoslavia, however, reopened the possibility of armed conflicts in the new state system in eastern Europe. This raises the issue of whether Europe really has moved beyond the age of war-fighting, or whether the Cold War was merely an interlude.

Approach and method

This study seeks to address several questions. First, in the light of rapid political and economic change, how should we conceive of the new European order? Second, how does the new order in Europe relate to underlying changes in the economic, political and security arenas, and to the changing pattern of relationships between international institutions, states and societies? And, third, how does the new order affect the prospects for cooperation and conflict among European societies and states?

The study approaches these questions with reference to three main themes:

(1) The tension between separate centres of power in an anarchic international system and efforts to construct institutions and norms which regulate this anarchy;
(2) The dynamic of economic integration and denser cross-national transactions, which engenders pressure for common political institutions but also generates resistance to integration;
(3) The changing relationship between state and society, and the ways in which different patterns of governance within societies condition relationships between them.

These themes need to be interpreted in the context of historical change. The dramatic changes since 1989 had a dynamic of their own, but they also reflect longer rhythms. For example, a transition appears to be taking place in the nature of the state in Europe. This is a very long-term process. There has also been a gradual shift in the structures of economic activity. The failure of communist regimes can be attributed, at least in part, to the obsolescence of a model of heavy industrial society which the advanced industrialized societies have left behind. Changes in governance and national identity reflect more long-term changes in the relationships between society and state.

Some of these changes can be interpreted usefully in evolutionary terms. A variety of political forms proliferates: some are selected as part of the mainstream; others are discarded. For example, the state has undergone many changes of form over time. From the dynastic principality of the early modern period there emerged mercantilist republics like the United Provinces, and absolutist states like France in the seventeenth and eighteenth centuries and Tsarist Russia. In the nineteenth century, nationalism and state structures came together to form the nation-state. This became the predominant form in the European state-system, and was reproduced on a large scale by the processes of colonization and decolonization. The twentieth century has produced the phenomena of the one-party state, the superpower, and the multi-state community. States representing different branches of historical evolution exist at the same time, creating complex international societies. The present order in Europe is certainly such a composite. Nevertheless, it may contain a main line of development for international society.

This chapter principally addresses the history of political orders in Europe since the nineteenth century, examining the continuities and discontinuities in the evolution of the present order. It is necessary first, however, to raise the question of what Europe is, and what areas, cultures and peoples it includes and excludes.

What is Europe?

Historically, Europe has always been a divided continent, but one with shared experiences and shared roots. Most Europeans share a common ancestry in the waves of migration and settlement into Europe in the early stone age, around −15,000. The languages they speak (with notable exceptions such as Finnish, Estonian and Hungarian) derive from a single origin, Indo-European, which had differentiated into nine major branches with many offshoots by the beginning of recorded history. The inhabitants of Europe developed many societies and cultures with their own traditions. Some of these have enjoyed long periods of continuity; others have been obliterated or lost. Migration and warfare have scattered peoples so that Europe is now a mosaic of cultures and languages.

Despite this diversity, distances in Europe are small relative to other culture-areas. Europe (especially western Europe) is well endowed with navigable rivers and coastlines, and long-distance travel by sea and river routes has been relatively easy. Consequently trade and cultural contacts have spread common styles and ideas throughout the European area. This has been true as far back as −3500 to −1500, when over a period of two thousand years, and across an area stretching around the European coast from Malta to Scandinavia, people erected stone circles and megalithic monuments of a similar style. The cultural influence of Rome extended far beyond the areas within the empire, so that Roman engineering, civil law and civic culture became a common heritage. Even in the fragmented conditions of the medieval period, religious ideas and institutions, art and architecture and music, traditions of technology, methods of industry and agriculture, patterns of urban settlement and administration were common over large areas. All Europe has shared the experience of Christian religion, and the importance of the Church as an institution in society.

But there have been important divergences, from an early time. Western Europe's experience includes the development of feudalism, the escape of the towns from aristocratic influence, and the rise of an independent class of town-dwelling traders and financiers. Elements of an open, commercial culture also existed in Bohemia, Poland and Hungary in the Middle Ages, but in most of eastern Europe serfdom persisted long after it had died out in the West. Invasions and conquests, from which western Europe was shielded, repeatedly disrupted east European societies. Subsequently the rule of the Ottoman, Habsburg and Russian empires interrupted the development of indigenous states and constrained the development of a dynamic urban trading culture such as that which developed in the West. Although eastern Europe was culturally more advanced in the early Middle Ages,[1] by the fifteenth century western and central Europe had become the source of most of the major cultural movements, such as the Renaissance, the scientific revolution, the enlightenment and the industrial revolution. It was western Christendom which launched the voyages of discovery and colonization which were to make western Europe the basis of the first world civilization, almost two hundred years before Peter the Great set about westernizing Russia.

The division of the Roman empire produced a basic line of cleavage between western and eastern Europe, which is mirrored in the differences between Latin and Orthodox Christianity; this has been one of the enduring divisions in Europe. The area under Muslim influence in southeastern Europe marked another. There are cleavages within western Europe too, such as between Protestant and Catholic Europe. But the gap between western and eastern cultures has been more persistent.

Culturally, then, Europe has elements which divide as well as elements which unite. Of course, Europeans share their heritage and culture with people in other geographical areas, notably the United States. What distinguishes Europe is a particular mix of social and cultural patterns within a single geographical area.

But geographically, too, Europe's boundaries are arbitrary. The Urals make a useful dividing line, and the area from the Atlantic to the Urals at least includes those European states which consider themselves to belong to the European state system, but the Urals do not constitute a social, cultural or even political divide. The area from Portugal to Poland is perhaps of more immediate relevance to the European Union, but Russia and the European republics of the former Soviet Union clearly play a critical part in the wider European arena. CSCE Europe, including the United States and Canada, also has political salience. This study therefore takes a wide focus, but gives most attention to developments in Europe up to the boundaries of the former Soviet Union.

Europe has never been politically united. Coercive attempts to unify the continent have ended in disaster. Indeed, the divisions of Europe have been one of the sources of its vitality and dynamism. The gulf which arose between the town and the traditional agricultural society was the source of the great expansion of trade in the later medieval period; and later it was the competition between trading states that stimulated Europe's expansion. In the world of ideas and beliefs, too, Europe has made progress through its divisions and schisms, in contrast to the accretive and synthesizing preferences of other cultures. Successive splits within Christianity, clashes between different views of the natural world and opposing political ideas, the conflict between capitalist and socialist models of political economy – all these have been characteristic of European culture.

This tradition of political disunity has made the question of political order a perennial problem in European history and, with the spread of the European state system, in the world. Ever since the system began to take its modern shape in the seventeenth century, the problem of how to manage Europe's anarchic international society has exercised thinkers. As military technology grew more destructive, and especially after the total wars of the twentieth century, the construction of a durable European (and world) order has become an issue of wide concern.

European orders, past and present
The following sections review the development of three aspects of the evolving European order from the nineteenth century to the present: the international political system, economic integration, and the state–society relationship. In this period, Europe has experienced a succession of political orders, each of which provided stability for a while, only to break up later. The sequence can be set out as below:[2]

1815 to 1854	Congress of Vienna system
1854 to 1871	Bismarck's wars
1871 to 1914	From the Concert of Europe to alliances
1914 to 1918	First World War
1918 to 1939	League of Nations
1939 to 1945	Second World War
1945 to 1989	Cold War
1989–	Post-Cold War era.

In each interwar period a structure of temporarily stable relations was erected which succeeded for a while in maintaining peace. On each occasion a revisionist power arose which refused to tolerate its position in the status quo or its exclusion by dominant powers. Since 1945, stable relations have been defined in terms of the two blocs; the end of this system in 1989 at first took place without major violence, but the war in Yugoslavia and the growing violence in the former Soviet Union suggest once again that a change of order tends to be marked by instability.

Despite the continuing existence of an anarchic order (in the sense of the absence of institutions with a global authority in the system), there has been an important and strengthening trend towards regulating and modifying this anarchy through the creation of *international institutions and international norms*.

A second factor which has influenced the pattern of anarchy, and seems likely to influence it more in the future, is the steady increase in *international economic integration*. This process took off in Europe in the nineteenth century, as the industrial revolution spread organically through the continent. This was a period when ideas, capital and entrepreneurs could move throughout Europe with little check. It was only towards the end of the nineteenth century, and more strongly in the early twentieth century, that protectionism began to slow the integration process. The First World War and the ideological divisions of the interwar period interrupted it again, and cut Russia off from the west European economy. After the Second World War, integration revived with renewed vigour in western Europe, but eastern Europe and the Soviet Union developed their own separate economic system. The end of the Cold War raises the possibility that the process which was developing at the end of the nineteenth century might recommence.

A third factor which has influenced the development of Europe's political orders has been the *differences between systems of governance* prevailing within states. The power of the state has grown enormously during this period, but the social base for political participation has also widened. As these two processes developed at different rates in different parts of Europe, a wide range of systems of governance existed at any one time. The tensions between them have been an important factor influencing the prospects for cooperation and conflict.

The Congress of Vienna system, 1815–54

As an international order, the Congress of Vienna system was remarkably stable and led to a relatively low level of international war during the nineteenth century. It was based on the preponderance in Europe of a relatively small number of Great Powers and agreement between them to preserve the international status quo. The prime aim of the governments of these powers was to resist further revolutionary incursions of the kind they had defeated in the Napoleonic wars. A secondary aim was to manage the international system in such a way as to preserve its stability. In Castlereagh's words, the purpose of the Concert was

> to inspire the States of Europe with a sense of the dangers they have surmounted by their union ... to make them feel that the existing Concert is their only perfect security against the revolutionary embers more or less existing in every state of Europe; and that their true wisdom is to keep down the petty contentions of ordinary times, and to stand together in support of the established principles of social order.[3]

The system had a common set of norms, which the members of the system tacitly accepted. The Great Powers maintained the Concert through conferences and congresses. They agreed to refrain from unilateral adjustments to the existing order. In particular they foreswore acts which were to the disadvantage of any particular power, or to the balance of power in general. Changes would have to be made by consent and consensus.

9

The system was designed to be unchanging, and it worked well while the assumptions on which it was established continued to hold. This was a period when social change was still relatively slow. In the early nineteenth century industrialization had yet to have its most powerful effect on the international system, and the social order remained oligarchic. In relatively democratic Great Britain, for example, only 600,000 male property-holders had the vote in 1832. But changes were on their way.

The industrial revolution spread through Europe in three waves.[4] In the first, up to about 1850, the new factories and industrial towns of Britain were at the core of the process, penetrating European markets widely with textiles, iron goods and other products. In the second, up to 1873, the industrial pattern of production spread to new centres, including Flanders, the northern French and Belgian coalfields, the Rhineland, upper Silesia, and St Petersburg. In the third, up to 1914, continental centres of production reached and in some cases overtook British ones, and areas like the Ruhr, the Paris basin, the Donetz and Lombardy supplied goods to and drew labour and resources from less developed regions.

Industrialization both integrated Europe and made it a smaller place. The spreading network of railways made it easier to trade across frontiers. At the same time as this integrated the European economy, it also integrated nations. The growth of large industrial cities began to create mass societies. Mass circulation newspapers and mass political parties provided the context for a new kind of national identity.

The eruption of nationalism into the tidy framework of the Great Power system was eventually to disrupt the international order. It led to the unification of Germany and Italy, and indirectly to Bismarck's wars against Denmark, Austria and France.

From the Concert of Europe to a Europe of alliances: the international order 1871–1914.

Even these shocks did not destroy the Congress system. They certainly breached its norms; but the Concert of Europe absorbed the new states and continued to survive until 1880. Bismarck's Germany was now at the centre of the system, but there was still a balance of power, which the members of the system continued to respect. When the British minister Buchanan warned Bismarck in 1863 that Europe would not allow Prussia to occupy Poland, Bismarck retorted, 'Who is Europe?' Buchanan replied, 'Several great nations', and Bismarck accepted the reply.[5]

European states were becoming more conscious of their national power, and more conscious of their rivalry. Outside Europe, they competed in the scramble for Africa and in the carve-up of China. Inside Europe, the Great Powers were more cautious, but their rivalry expressed itself in the manoeuvring over the Eastern Question, and in the build-up of armaments, which began to pour out of new arms industries across the continent.[6] All the Great Powers began to enter defensive alliances, and no further congresses were held after 1878. The Powers were no longer willing to act on the basis of a shared interest in European security. As governments made common cause with the nationalism of their own states, they lost their earlier sense of a common threat. Accordingly insecurity grew, and diplomatic rivalry intensified. This became dangerous when it involved the interests of the Great Powers in regions of instability, such as the Balkans.

For a while the trend towards economic integration continued, even though the political order was beginning to fragment. Europe as a whole was expanding its economy rapidly, and its products were penetrating the rest of the world. This was the period when European companies and states established highly favourable and unequal economic relations with the non-industrialized periphery. In Europe, the predominance of the industrial centres and the flood of cheap imported food from outside the continent weakened the old agricultural regions. The response was the growth of protectionism.

In western Europe, as industrialization and urbanization brought new social groups into political systems throughout the nineteenth century, the demand for political participation was met by extensions of the suffrage. In central Europe, the social demand for participation expressed itself in demands for national unification, which was to lead to differences with other national groups. In eastern Europe, where peasant societies predominated, demands for participation expressed themselves as movements for national freedom and social revolution.

The nineteenth-century order broke down, eventually, because the Great Powers lost their sense of solidarity. By 1914, discontent with the existing balance of power had grown. The international system was polarized into alliances of heavily armed powers. The integration of economic activity had led to a phase of nationalist competition rather than to political integration. The threat posed by nationalism to the old multinational empire of Austria–Hungary was sufficient to light the fuse.

The interwar period and the League of Nations

The impact of the First World War on the old system was shattering. Three Great Powers (the Ottoman empire, Russia and Austria–Hungary) were knocked out of the system. An extra-European power (the United States) for the first time played a decisive role in European affairs. The war left France and Italy weakened. Britain was never to recover its pre-1914 greatness and Germany was near collapse. The war also had a devastating effect on the European economy. Although recovery was fairly fast, the integrated economic order did not revive.

The trauma of the war and its massive human and physical costs profoundly affected European attitudes. The victors recoiled from the prospect of having to repeat their ordeal; hence the rhetoric about 'the war to end war', and the determination of the Big Three – Britain, France and the United States – to construct an order to prevent its recurrence. President Woodrow Wilson could 'predict with absolute certainty that within another generation there will be another world war if the nations of the world do not concert methods to prevent it.'[7] He regarded the militaristic, secretive and undemocratic practices of the Great Powers as the root cause of the war, and he was determined to impose a new order on the basis of idealist principles. Collective security was once more to underpin the new order, but this time through a new international organization, and on the basis of a set of agreed principles.

In the long term these ideas were to be influential, but in 1919 the other victors disagreed with Wilson. Clemenceau was much more interested in a punitive settlement that would prevent the re-emergence of German power. Lloyd George saw the new order as a continuation of the old. He was prepared to be lenient with Germany, but he thought the Great Powers would go on managing the system as they always had. Accordingly the League was set up as a compromise between an international organization with universal pretensions, and a system for maintaining the dominance of the victors over the vanquished. It was to fulfil neither aim. The strength of isolationism in America, and the exclusion of Bolshevik Russia, undermined the first. The latent strength of Germany undermined the second.

The norms of the new order were based on the principles of collective security, disarmament, reference of crises to the League, and self-determination. The French wanted to give the League majority voting and strong powers of coercion, but the British resisted this as an encroachment upon sovereignty. The League therefore operated on the basis of unanimity; as in the Concert system, there was no effective provision for action when unanimity broke down. The League could be successful, sometimes, in managing small disputes, but it had limited tools for managing conflicts between major states and it had no tools at all for managing the new type of conflict that was breaking over the international system: the clash of incompatible ideologies.

In eastern and central Europe, the principle of self-determination led to the creation of eight new states, five taken from western Russia, three from the old Austro-Hungarian empire. They were to be a weak and divided group of states between Germany and Russia.

The interwar political order might have been better able to adapt and survive if its economic foundations had been sounder. For a while, in the 1920s, the liberal trading system was restored, and the economy boomed. But European governments were in debt following the war, the dollar was overvalued, and tariffs were starting to rise. The German economy, saddled with reparations, debt and inflation, was in a particularly grave condition, weakening the economy of Europe as a whole. As the Wall Street crash reverberated through Europe, creating unemployment and protectionism, political systems began to buckle under the strain. Europe faced all at once the rise of the fascist movements, the threat of rearmament and demands for the revision of international borders. The interwar order was unable to survive these challenges. With the resources of Germany at his disposal, Hitler set out on his course of systematic destruction. For a brief but terrible period, the triumphant order in Europe was militaristic fascism, from the Atlantic coast to the Urals.

1945–89: The division of Europe

The effects of the Second World War on the European order were even more dramatic and sweeping than those of the First. After the defeat of Germany, the United States and the Soviet Union eclipsed the European powers. This time, there was to be no agreed postwar order, for there was little the victors could agree about, other than the recognition of one another's spheres of interest. With central and eastern Europe swept into the command economy, and West Germany and other western states integrated into an American-dominated economic system, Europe was more rigidly divided than ever before.

In western Europe economic integration gathered pace again. The coming of mass transport and air travel shrank Europe once more. Industrial concentration and economies of scale meant that large plants and companies could supply European and world markets. Multinational

13

companies, already developing rapidly in the interwar period, increased their numbers and influence; this was one of the factors which bound western Europe into the world market economy.

In eastern Europe, Stalin imposed a kind of quasi-integration through Comecon and the Warsaw Pact. The regimes organized economic activity in such a way as to promote the heavy-industrial pattern of development that the Soviet Union had itself pioneered. While the communist regimes dominated politics and excluded effective participation by non-communists, the powers of the state became so swollen that most economic activity became a branch of state administration.

These divergent trends meant that western and eastern Europe developed different systems of economic and political integration, with economic organization following the lines of security systems. Indeed, the political order had effectively controlled and diverted the pattern of economic integration.

However, a number of trends overlaid and complicated the Cold War pattern, and already began to sow the seeds of a different order.

The first was the growing economic strength of western Europe relative to the United States. A turning-point came in the late 1960s and 1970s. Before this time, the United States was the dominant economic as well as military partner, and US leadership was clear in multilateral regimes such as the Bretton Woods system and GATT. After 1971 the US trading balance went into deficit. The system of fixed exchange rates, pegged to a strong dollar, collapsed in 1973. The oil shocks of 1973 and 1979 opened sharp policy differences between the US and European states. Conflicts over trade, foreign policy and defence continued throughout the 1980s and into the 1990s. Meanwhile the US share in world trade gradually fell relative to that of the west Europeans.

Secondly, the development of the EC created a political framework for further west European integration. The Community gathered impetus through the 1980s, with the strengthening of intergovernmental political cooperation, the easing of budgetary disputes, and the Single European Act. Member states increasingly coordinated foreign policy, and sought EC backing for their foreign policy positions. Despite its internal tensions, the EC had come to be seen as one of the major actors on the world stage.

Within western Europe, Germany was gradually coming to translate its economic strength into political influence. German governments pursued an active foreign policy, which was gradually to reshape Europe. First, Adenauer's *Westpolitik* tied Germany closely to France, then

Brandt's *Ostpolitik* opened the way for cooperation with the Soviet Union and the GDR. These initiatives laid the groundwork for the Helsinki process and contributed to the easing of tensions with the Soviet Union.

The CSCE process grew out of the Cold War, but it also pointed forward to the new political order. Initially a bargain between the Soviet desire for recognition of existing frontiers and the western desire for Soviet observance of human rights, it elaborated a new set of norms for interstate behaviour in Europe. Operating by consensus and conferences, the CSCE has striking resonances with the Concert system.

The existence of nuclear weapons also forced on their holders norms of a kind, or at least tacit rules of non-engagement. They included the mutual recognition of relatively clear-cut geographical and political boundaries, and great caution about allowing direct conflict between conventional forces of nuclear powers. The danger of unregulated competition drove the superpowers into arms control, and eventually to hot lines, crisis management, summits, and a steadily more involved process of mutual security management. The outcome of this was eventually to be agreements on conventional forces, confidence-building measures, verification, and exchange of information between military forces.

Despite its apparent rigidity, then, even the Cold War security structure was showing signs of movement, from an anarchic towards a managed system.

Other links were developing between east and west. Trade grew in the 1980s. Despite political restrictions, such as the Coordinating Committee on Export Controls (CoCom), it was important to both sides. The Soviet Union imported food and technological products; western Europe imported Soviet energy.

The east European countries could not easily escape from the constraints of their economic system. Inefficient use of labour, waste, high energy intensity and heavy pollution were endemic, resulting from the emphasis on planned output targets irrespective of inputs. Resistant to innovation, and weak in local management skills, their economies eventually became incapable even of sustaining existing patterns of growth. Attempts to reform and modernize the system failed repeatedly, because of their political and ideological implications. Khrushchev's attempt contributed to his ousting; Dubcek's led to the invasion of Czechoslovakia in 1968 and the installation of a hard-line government. Later reforms decentralized economic management but still failed to deliver strong economic growth.[8]

The communist regimes in eastern Europe grew more corrupt and demoralized. Dissidents organized civic movements of protest, often at great personal cost. They took strength from contacts with social movements in the West; such contacts were particularly important in the two Germanies. In Poland, Solidarity's resistance to government repression and economic failure set off the sequence of events which brought about the downfall of the communist regimes.

The post-Cold War order

Following the fall of the Berlin Wall, events gathered speed: the communist regimes in eastern Europe collapsed, Germany proceeded to rapid unification and the EC member states decided to accelerate the European Union. The Soviet Union disintegrated, producing a large number of new states in the former Soviet space. Yugoslavia broke up violently and Czechoslovakia divided peacefully.

Progress towards a European Union faltered when the Danish population narrowly rejected the Treaty on European Union. The French endorsed it with an equally narrow margin. The British parliamentary ratification process took eighteen months and was not completed until the Prime Minister threatened rebels in his own party with a general election. The German ratification was delayed even longer by a court challenge. By the time that eventual ratification seemed assured, most of the political impetus of the step towards Union had been lost. Sweden, Finland, Austria and Norway decided to apply to join the EC, but it remained unclear whether their populations would approve and whether the negotiations would succeed in time for the 1996 Intergovernmental Conference. The Swiss reasserted their long tradition of independence by voting to stay out of the European Economic Area. Nationalism grew in western as well as eastern Europe, and in Italy regional divisions and the decay of old parties completely changed the political system.

The dynamic processes that have been released in Europe since 1989 are clearly still under way, and therefore it is more appropriate to speak about an emergent European order than one that has been settled. Uncertainties about its future shape are still strong. For example, it is still unclear whether Europe will move towards closer cooperation with its major trading partners in the triad, or whether a shift towards greater protectionism will accompany the formation of trading blocs.

In the EC, further integration and consolidation of existing structures are possible and so is fragmentation. The process of widening could be halted by the present upheavals, and the EC could even narrow to a core group prepared to undertake the final stages of monetary and economic union. Alternatively the EC could widen to include some or all of the current and potential applicants: the EFTA states, the Visegrad group,* Slovenia, Bulgaria and Romania, the Baltic States, the southern European states (Cyprus, Malta and Turkey), and the other Yugoslav states, and potentially even some of the newly independent republics of the former Soviet Union. The east European reform process could succeed or fail in different states, and Russia could emerge from its present turmoil into a process of democratic reform, or slip into authoritarian rule.

Out of this *mélange* of uncertainties, it is possible to take three sharply defined scenarios as points of orientation for discussing trends. The first is *Fragmented Europe*. In this scenario European Union fails, the Franco-German axis breaks, reforms are relatively unsuccessful in eastern Europe, and there is a return to fractious nation-states in both western and eastern Europe. The second is *Fortress Western Europe:* in this scenario the European Union becomes a basis for a strongly integrated EC, which might expand to take in the EFTA states, but reforms in eastern Europe are relatively unsuccessful and the west Europeans are reluctant to offer EC membership to new applicants after the EFTA states and maintain barriers against migration and trade from eastern Europe and other areas on the periphery of the EC. The third scenario is *Wider Europe*, in which a way is found to extend the process of developing cooperation and integration, based on a reformed EC and other European institutions, with the societies of eastern and perhaps southeastern Europe. A fourth scenario might be Atlantic Europe: close links between western Europe and North America based on security and trade cooperation; but this can be taken as a variant of the Wider Europe or Fortress Europe scenarios. Of course the real shape of events will be less simple than these sketches, but these extremes help to provide landmarks for considering how different trends are affecting change. First, however, it is necessary to establish a conceptual frame of reference, and this is the task to which the next chapter turns.

*Hungary, Poland, the Czech Republic and Slovakia.

2

PARADIGMS AND PARADOXES: THE SHAPE OF THE NEW EUROPE

The upheavals in the European landscape have shifted mental as well as territorial boundaries. Frames of reference which appeared to be valid for the Cold War period no longer hold. Europeans appeared to lack a vision and a sense of direction about the future of their continent. The uncertainty about what Europe comprises is a symptom of this confusion. The basis of 'order' is unclear in the new Europe, and consequently the role of different international institutions remains undefined.

Old paradigms of international relations no longer seem satisfactory. In the Cold War, three largely separate groups of scholars wrote about the East–West conflict, the west European integration process, and the politics of the former Soviet bloc. History has driven western and eastern Europe together, but a common theoretical framework for interpreting events in the wider Europe does not yet exist.

At one level, this is not surprising, since unlike natural scientists, who change paradigms when contrary evidence overwhelms a framework of explanation,[1] the community of scholars of international relations is content to hold several paradigms at once for long periods, and individual scholars sometimes combine at least two paradigms in their own writings. As the development and interaction of large societies is undoubtedly complex and poorly understood, it is appropriate to regard a paradigm as a partial view of reality. Multiple paradigms may then be helpful, for, like the elephant illuminated by the torchlight of several close observers, the same phenomenon may make more sense if different partial views are put together.

History is constantly changing, so yesterday's paradigm may no longer be wholly appropriate today. But history changes in a gradual, evolutionary way, building new layers on the old. Elements of a new order in Europe are visible, but not yet established, and elements of the old order are still in evidence. It is therefore unlikely that any single paradigm will be wholly satisfactory in a transitional period. Older paradigms may still have value but newer ones should reflect emerging realities.

This chapter reviews theoretical notions of 'order' and attempts to indicate their relevance to contemporary European conditions. A specific focus is on how the order, in the sense of the arrangement of states, societies and international institutions in Europe, affects 'order', in the sense of inducing cooperation and limiting conflict at the international and domestic levels. The starting assumption is that events since 1989 reflect not only a redistribution of power and territory, but a deeper change in the relationships between international institutions, societies and states.

This chapter first reviews concepts of order implicit in the realist, interdependence, integrationist and liberal-pluralist perspectives, and then goes on to sketch a conceptual framework for the study based on the interdependence and liberal-pluralist approach. Finally it suggests a connection between the structure of the international society in Europe and the scenarios outlined at the end of the previous chapter.

States, anarchy and international order

From a realist perspective, the basic institution of the international system is the sovereign state. The 180-odd states are the constituent legal personalities of international society. According to the norms of this society, which are reflected in international law, each state is responsible for jurisdiction in its own territory; each is the supreme law-making authority, holding the monopoly of legitimate force, upholding the rule of law and domestic order, and authoritatively allocating resources and values within its society. Between states, order is more fragile, given the absence of a supreme authority and the unwillingness of some states to accommodate the interests of others. Nevertheless, international order can exist to some degree, insofar as states observe common norms and act in such a way as to preserve themselves individually and collectively.

Hedley Bull, who made the classic statement from a realist position, argued that an international order should be seen as 'a pattern of activity that sustains the elementary or primary goals of the society of states, or international society'.[2] These goals are, first, the preservation of the system of states itself, second, the preservation of the independence and sovereignty of individual states and, third, the maintenance of peace. One of the chief ways through which states uphold order is by maintaining a balance of power.

Bull goes on to discuss the possibility of mitigating anarchy by developing an 'international society'. This exists 'when a group of states, conscious of certain common interests and common values, form a society in the sense that they conceive themselves to be bound by a common set of rules in their relations with one another, and share in the workings of common institutions' (such as respect for international law, diplomatic conventions and the customs and conventions of war). The stronger the international society, the less disorderly international relations are likely to be.

Bull accepts that non-state actors such as businesses, television companies, political parties and churches operate a 'transnational nexus' which may affect international relations, and that the 'world political process' cannot be understood solely in terms of interstate politics. A 'world order' (or world society) is developing which differs from the international order in that the interstate system is only part of this order, and the purpose of the world order is not the preservation of states but the sustenance of 'social life among mankind as a whole'. However, Bull questioned whether a world society had yet developed with 'a sense of common interest and common values, on the basis of which common rules and institutions may be built.' Bull's concept can inform a notion of a European order, which would build a European 'international society' on common interests and values.

Globalization, regimes and complex interdependence

In the postwar period, and especially since the 1970s, a new wave of modernization has begun to affect west European societies, as well as the societies in the United States, Japan, and other OECD states. It has been characterized by a set of economic and technological changes in these advanced industrial societies which have led to increased economic and technological interdependence and interpenetration. These changes include the development of the world economy, in which production and investment are oriented to international rather than domestic markets; the establishment of virtually instantaneous communications across the globe; and the diffusion of similar technologies which have had a homogenizing effect on the societies which have adopted them. This phenomenon ('globalization') has had important consequences for the relationship between state and society and for international relations. First, it meant a steady increase in the importance of multilateral, as compared with bilateral, diplomacy, and a concomitant growth in institutions and regimes to manage areas of interdependence. Second, it put a premium on the ability to influence collective decisions – so that influence within an institution or a regime grew more important relative to classical measures of state power, and bargaining power grew more important relative to coercive power in warfare. Third, it meant the emergence of a new layer of governance, above (or between) states. States became less autonomous in their home societies, but gained wider influence and policy scope internationally, as they dealt collectively with issues beyond their borders through international institutions.

Institutions and regimes are likely to be of particular importance in conditions of 'complex interdependence', where states are vulnerable and sensitive to one another's actions. Keohane and Nye proposed 'complex interdependence' as an alternative model to realism, to describe international systems in which the progress of globalization was advanced. They proposed their model of complex interdependence as an ideal type, but argued that in some 'issue-areas' the model works better than realist assumptions. An 'issue-area' is defined as a policy area where policy-makers perceive links between the issues: 'When the governments active on a set of issues see them as closely interdependent, and deal with them collectively, we call that set of issues an issue-area'.[3] Thus, for example, monetary policy is an international issue-area. Their model is an attempt to explain international relations in those issue-areas which meet the three conditions of complex interdependence:

(1) Multiple channels connect societies (interstate, transgovernmental, transnational);
(2) 'The agenda of international relations consists of multiple issues that are not arranged in a clear or consistent hierarchy. This absence of hierarchy among issues means, among other things, that military security does not consistently dominate the agenda';
(3) 'Military force is not used by governments toward other governments within the region, or on the issues, when complex interdependence prevails.'

The idea of a regime as a set of 'implicit or explicit principles, norms, rules and decision-making procedures, around which actors' expectations converge in a given area of international relations'[4] has been accepted both by neo-realists and by interdependence theorists. Clearly, the more regime-like the international system becomes, the less it takes the character of an anarchy, and the greater the prospects for international order.

There is disagreement, however, about the conditions under which regimes and institutions can survive. Neo-realists see the state as the focus of vital interests, and argue that regimes will last only so long as states require them to mitigate the disbenefits of uncoordinated action. Some also argue that a hegemon is necessary for a regime to work.

'Neo-liberal institutionalists', in contrast, argue that institutions can modify states' perceptions of their interests and take on a life of their own as an additional layer of governance. This debate affects expectations of the future of the European Community, for neo-realists[5] tend to view cooperation within the EC as a product of a bipolar period and expect it to break up following the end of the Cold War, while neo-liberal institutionalists[6] argue that states need institutions such as the EC to fulfil their own purposes and expect it both to survive and to shape states' interests.[7]

If we accept that a situation approximating 'complex interdependence' exists in western Europe and the OECD, how far east does this zone extend? For much of the Cold War period, globalization had a limited effect in eastern Europe. Communist regimes sought to maintain closed and autarkic societies, and actively resisted the diffusion of technologies such as the telephone and the computer which were essential elements of the 'networked' industrial society in the West. When eventually economic decline forced a choice between continued stagnation and reform, the choice of reform was to prove too threatening for communist regimes to survive. In this sense, globalization has been an underlying factor in both the integration process in western Europe and the disintegration process in eastern Europe. However, globalization has still not penetrated very far in east European societies, and they are more dependent on international financial institutions and western trade and investment than interdependent with western Europe. The issue of the use of force is still on the agenda in relations between states in the former Soviet Union and eastern Europe, and it has not been definitively removed from East–West relations.

Therefore, it cannot be said that 'complex interdependence' prevails in the wider Europe; rather, a region of 'complex interdependence' adjoins a region with a traditional anarchic state system. The issue is how relations will develop between these regions. One possibility is that anarchy will be the stronger force, and that western Europe will behave in a state-like way in its relations with east European states, defending its own interests with little attempt at cooperation; or turmoil in eastern Europe might disrupt existing frameworks for cooperation in western Europe. Another possibility is that interdependence will be the stronger force, and that east European states will be drawn into cooperative frameworks with the west Europeans, in which the EC might or might not play the role of a hegemon. The logic of the interdependence position argues for constructing order by extending complex interdependence (for example by investment and trade) and by establishing cooperative regimes to manage issue-areas of common concern.

European integration

Globalization has been particularly powerful in western Europe, because of the relative smallness of states and the density of their transactions in a small continent. Among EC member states its effects combined powerfully with the existing project of regional economic integration. The development of the EC as a partly supranational, partly intergovernmental system has created a new order in western Europe, which goes well beyond a regime. West European states no longer operate in a condition of anarchy, since they have accepted the authority of EC law and of the EC Council of Ministers in crucial areas of policy. The Treaty of European Union makes clear the scale of changes that these states are prepared to accept. If the declared aspirations of coordinated economic and monetary management, home and foreign and security policies come into effect, it will be unclear whether the appropriate model for analysing the European Community should be drawn from international politics or from internal politics. Certainly west European politics can no longer be analysed only in terms of relations between states; relations between the EC, states and sub-national bodies, and between sub-national bodies themselves, also have to be taken into account.

Jean Monnet and his colleagues saw European integration as a means of achieving a new west European order, which would have the aim of eliminating the threat of war among its members, leading eventually to a European federation. Starting with an economic agreement over the coal and steel industries, formerly the basis for armaments, they hoped to develop an 'ever closer union' through successive measures of functional cooperation. This scheme met much resistance and many delays, but has nevertheless made great progress over time. As a result of long bargaining, slow convergence of expectations, and common interests with respect to the world economy, the governments of EC states have incrementally extended the scope of their integration and cooperation to new issue-areas. It is evident that the process remains uneven and incomplete.

With the future of integration still in doubt, the EC moved on to enlargement. As its members gradually forged the EC as a vehicle for their interests, new members had to adapt to the interests of existing members. Accession is abrupt, compared with integration, and new members have had to accept the *acquis communautaire* with little room for bargaining. The enlargement process thus has a different dynamic from the integration process, and the EC acts more like a hegemon than an equal partner in relation to applicant members. Once inside, however, new members can take their part in the internal bargaining and decision-making and if successful (as in the case of Spain) can establish strong positions.

Deutsch,[8] Haas,[9] Nye[10] and others have discussed the conditions which favour successful integration. Deutsch, for example, identifies compatible values and expectations, anticipation of economic gains, ready communications between political elites and between elites and societies, mobility of people between the territories concerned, multiple transactions, and mutually predictable behaviour as conditions for the establishment of integrated political communities ('amalgamated security communities'). Less stringent conditions were required for 'pluralistic security communities', which did not develop common government but lost the fear of fighting one another; according to his findings, these require only complementary elite values and mutually responsive governments.

Whether the east European societies meet the conditions for integration is an open question. There appears to be a good measure of concordance of elite values in most cases, around the basic western political values of multi-party democracy and open markets. Deeper down there are differences in political cultures, public attitudes and the institutions of civil society. Similar differences existed between EC members and the Mediterranean applicants before their accession.

Some integration theorists argue that the success of the EC rests on a delicate balance between the Community institutions, the state and society which has evolved over a long time, and that rapid expansion to include societies which lack this balance would destroy the Community.[11] Others argue that enlargement is inevitable and the EC must adjust.[12]

In principle, integration is a conclusive answer to the problems of anarchy, since the formation of a common political community should eliminate international conflict among the former units. However, integration may also internalize or suppress conflicts rather than resolve them (as in the case of the former Yugoslavia) and integrated communities may later disintegrate. Deutsch found that amalgamated security communities were more unstable and prone to violent disintegration than pluralistic security communities.[13] As he points out, the steps necessary for creating a pluralistic security community are less demanding than those for political integration. This would suggest that a form of association short of full political integration might be both a more feasible aim for extending the Community and a basis for a more stable organization.

Transnationalism and the liberal-pluralist theory

Closely related to integration theories is the liberal-pluralist theory, which takes a wider view of international relations than one based only or even mainly on states. In this paradigm, international cooperation depends not only on agreements between states and on institutions and regimes, but also on the compatibility of societies; hence compatible values and political processes, tolerance and mutual understanding are as important as international institutions, and it follows that transnational relations between non-state actors need attention as well as interstate relations. International society is made up not only of states, but of societies, each with their own expectations, identities, values and rules. A well-tempered order is one in which the arrangements within and between societies are sufficiently congruent that societies can express their diverse values and needs without undue conflict.

A multi-level society

Globalization and regional integration are bringing about deep changes in the relationships of states to one another and of societies to states. The old order of nation-states is being modified on the one hand by regimes and institutions which to some degree pool the powers of individual states, and on the other by nations untied to states. There is thus an emergent European order in two senses: in the geopolitical sense, and in the social order of the international society.

Interdependence has increased between societies as well as states, and non-state actors engage in transactions across borders and are sensitive and vulnerable to one another's actions. They include not only multi-national corporations but also local governments, professional associations, regions and cities, news media, churches, trade unions and citizens' movements.

If domestic interests in one state are strongly affected by national decisions in another (for example, farming interests by trade talks, English home-owners by German interest rates), a new interplay develops between domestic and foreign policy. The interests of foreign firms located in a host country may conflict with domestic interests, so that formerly international conflicts take on a domestic element, and formerly domestic conflicts can become internationalized. Conflict across levels can therefore become entangled with conflicts across countries.

In a schematic nineteenth-century world, national interests represented the interests of the dominant elite within the state. In the interdependent world of the late twentieth century, new alignments are developing, with states forming international regimes and organizations at other levels forming cross-national interest groups. This process could eventually lead to an integrated polity, but in the meantime it gives rise to an international society with different patterns of conflict and cooperation.

In such a system, political coalitions operate across states as well as within states. Issue-areas become the focus of other actors besides states. As Keohane and Nye write: 'For international regimes to govern situations of complex interdependence successfully, they must be congruent with the interests of powerfully placed domestic groups within major states, as well as with the structure of power among states.'[14] In a multi-level society domestic groups operate across borders and therefore regimes (or coalitions) of both domestic groups and states become important. Interdependent societies are also more open to waves of social change, political movements and similar social patterns.

This schematic presentation may oversimplify and exaggerate the extent of the change, but its direction is unmistakable. In western Europe as a whole, a multi-level international society is evolving, with relatively strong regimes and institutions, states and cross-national interest groups. This process is tending to moderate the level of conflict between states, and to redirect it between levels.

In eastern Europe, however, newly emergent states correspond more closely to the two-level, nineteenth-century model. Both states and societies are weak. Nevertheless the west European pattern exerts a strong influence. East European governments are drawn towards west European regimes, and east European societies are drawn into transnational patterns of social activity – for example, nationalist movements cooperate across borders, and human rights movements work closely with western groups. This transnational climate therefore affects the new nation-states.

The relative strength of international organizations, states and societies will influence the direction Europe takes with regard to the scenarios sketched in Chapter 1. Weak international organizations in western and eastern Europe, with strong states linked to societies which remain national rather than transnational, will tend to generate a fragmented Europe, an order in which violent conflict could be expected. Strong international organizations and open societies in western Europe, combined with weak international organizations and nationalist societies in eastern Europe, will tend towards a 'fortress' western Europe. This could provide a basis for a strengthened (and defensive) Community in western Europe, but for fragmentation in eastern Europe. International organizations which are strong across both western and eastern Europe, combined with societies that are oriented transnationally, offer a basis for the development of a Wider Europe, which in principle could provide a security community extending to east European societies.

3

1989 AND 1992: TOWARDS A EUROPEAN ECONOMIC SPACE?

The years 1989 and 1992 were turning-points in economic as well as political history. In eastern Europe, the collapse of communism heralded the end of the division of the European economy into two separate economic systems. In western Europe, the advent of the Single Market marked the integration of national economies into a single trading area. It was hoped at first that these two processes might open the way for a single economic space throughout Europe. In principle this would release the considerable economic potential of eastern Europe to the benefit of western Europe and the world economy, as well as attracting investment and trade into eastern Europe and raising living standards there. A common economic space would then open the way for the establishment of a common system of market democracy, membership of the European Community, the extension to eastern Europe of the west European security community, and the reintegration of the continent.

Another, less benign, scenario was also possible. Economic reform in eastern Europe might run into difficulties, west Europeans might be unwilling to invest there, and new economic walls could divide the continent between a region of prosperity in the EC and a group of failed economies in the East. Economic insecurity in eastern Europe might then ferment political instability and contribute to its fragmentation and destabilization, with consequences that might spill over into the security arena.

The course that Europe takes between these extremes depends in turn on three sets of factors, which this chapter will explore. The first is the place that Europe takes in the world economy, and whether the world

Figure 3.1   Relative size of European economies, by GDP, 1989

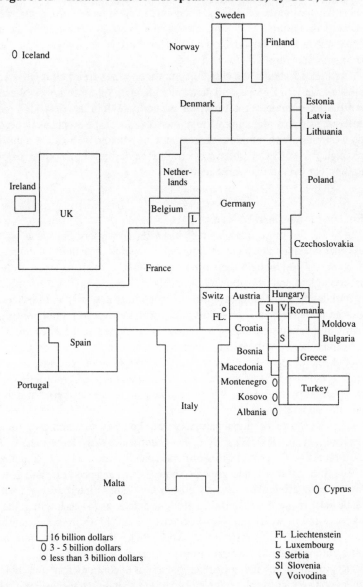

Source: Per Magnus Wijkman, *Structural Change in European Production and Trade*, EFTA Secretariat (Paper for Symposium on Europe into the Third Millenium), April 1992.

economy remains an open system or divides into protectionist blocs. The second is the course of regional economic integration in Europe, and the success or failure of the societies in the West in coordinating their economic and social development. The third is the progress of the economic transition in eastern Europe.

As Fig. 3.1 shows, the east European economies are small relative to those of western Europe, and per capita incomes are much lower. Western Europe dominates the European economy both in its size and in the emerging pattern of economic relationships: the east Europeans depend on western Europe for market access and investment, taking only a three per cent share of EC exports; western Europe depends more on its major trading partners in the world economy.

Europe in the world economy

The process of globalization which has affected western Europe as well as other developed economies is linked to a series of changes in the real economy. They include increasing automation, a sharp increase in the technological sophistication of products and production, a shift from materials-intensive to research-intensive content in goods and services, and an increase in the versatility and specialization of production.[1] In many of the major technological industries (cars, aerospace, telecommunications, heavy engineering, chemicals, etc.), markets have become global, and product development and production are increasingly drawn from specialized plants situated in different countries. The progress of this process of internationalization can be gauged from patterns of trade and investment.

Fig. 3.2 shows the global pattern of trade between western Europe and other regions in 1990. West European countries took the largest share of world trade – 58.6 per cent of world merchandise trade.[2] Throughout the 1980s, international trade grew at about 7 per cent per year, and both intra- and interregional trade have been increasing.[3] Interregional trade (especially to the West Pacific) is growing at least as fast as intraregional trade, or faster, which suggests that until the late 1980s, regionalization was not leading to a restraint on world trade. However, the share of intraregional trade in western Europe's total trade has increased.

Regionalization and globalization are not contradictory but twin phenonomena: greater interdependence and expanding trade are creating tighter links between countries both within and across regions. Transnational companies play an important role in maintaining these

Figure 3.2   World trade flows, 1990

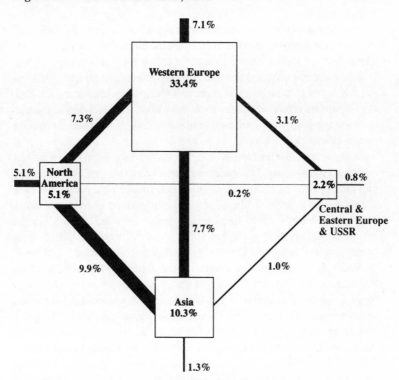

The figures show percentage shares of world merchandise trade (based on value) within regions, between regions, and with the rest of the world. Trade of region A with region B is defined as the sum of A's exports to B and B's exports to A.
Source: GATT International Trade, 1990–91, vol. 2, Table III.3, p. 9.

links. In the early 1980s, they accounted for more than 30 per cent of international trade among developed economies, much of it intra-firm;[4] by the early 1990s, the figure had risen to 60 per cent.

Investment has become even more important than trade as an index of the interlocking structure of economic activity. World foreign direct investment grew by 144 per cent between 1960 and 1980, and by a further 66 per cent between 1981 and 1988.[5] Large companies in all the leading sectors sought to establish themselves in the world's major markets. In the 1960s, large-scale investment into Europe was associated with the period of rapid expansion of US multinational companies. In the

1980s, there was a sharp growth in outward foreign direct investment from Europe.[6]

As national economies became interdependent in the world economy, they became more exposed to events outside the national state's control. The major economies tended to move together into growth or recession; and they became exposed to mutual policy effects and shocks. This was not a new phenomenon, but it grew in importance with internationalization. It was therefore necessary to manage this interdependence, if unco-ordinated or conflicting policies were not to cause economies to damage one another.

In the immediate postwar period, the United States played the leading coordinating role, and US trade and macroeconomic policies were crucial factors shaping the policy environment for the west Europeans. The United States pursued a liberal policy of investment in western Europe and had a healthy trade surplus, and both sides benefited from the relationship. However, in the late 1960s and early 1970s, as the US trade balance deteriorated and Germany and Japan challenged US economic primacy, the US hegemony declined. The turning-point was the abandonment of the Bretton Woods monetary system in 1973. The dollar floated and west Europeans began to concert with one another in an effort to re-establish exchange-rate stability; this led to the 'Snake' in 1972. Divergent responses to the oil shocks led to further differences between the United States and the Europeans, with disagreements too among the Europeans themselves. By the late 1970s, West Germany had begun to emphasize the development of a (west) European monetary area, in order to provide an environment favourable to its own policies, and a cushion against the vagaries of US policies.[7] As a massive US deficit built up in the later period of the Reagan administration, Europeans were again cautious of US policies and regarded regional economic integration as a preferable alternative. In this way, western Europe's relationship with the United States moved gradually from dependence to independence.

As the EC grew in strength as a trading bloc, and its economy became comparable in weight to that of the United States, the relationship became one combining partnership and rivalry. Conflicts of interest developed over trade and economic policy. The prolonged delay in negotiating the GATT round in 1992–3 and west European concern over the US deficit illustrate these differences. The Transatlantic Declaration, signed by the EC and the US, expressed support for integrating economic goals and closer consultation between their policy-making institutions, although the EC was unwilling to include the US in joint policy-making meetings.[8] While favouring cooperation, the United States became concerned that a more inward-looking EC might ignore American interests; certainly the coordination of policies among EC members weakened US influence in Europe and internationally among the G-7.

Similarly, Japan and the EC signed a joint declaration of cooperation at the Hague in July 1991, but Japan remained concerned that the strengthening of the EC would threaten exports of Japanese goods. The multilateral bodies, such as the G-7, the GATT, the International Monetary Fund (IMF) and the OECD, coordinate different aspects of policy; but they are relatively weak, intergovernmental regimes. Common interests in avoiding protectionism and coordinating sustainable development outweigh conflicting interests, but in a climate of recession, with domestic interests hankering for protection, such common interests cannot be guaranteed to prevail. The US has lost economic hegemony, the EC is not ready to fulfil a leadership role, and Japan is unable to do so. The relationships within the Triad have therefore become unstable, although mutual economic interests and interdependence hold it together.

West European trends
While developments in the world economy have thus created an incentive for west European integration, economic and political forces within western Europe have driven a process of regional economic integration which continues to have a decisive influence on the political order within Europe as a whole. Although western Europe remains very diverse, with important national and regional variations, a cohesive trading area and a single economic space have emerged. Three trends in particular have gathered strength in recent years: the emergence of a west European economy out of the individual national economies, the development of the EC as the regional economic hegemon, and the gradual increase in the policy scope of the EC.

The growing cohesion of the west European economy is evident in changing patterns of trade. Wijkman's analysis of trade flows[9] reveals three groups of countries in 1958: 'Core Europe', consisting of the EC-6,* together with Austria and Switzerland, clustering around Germany; the 'Northern Periphery', consisting of the UK and the Nordic states, for which the UK was the major partner; and the 'Southern Periphery', comprising Spain, Portugal, Greece, Yugoslavia and Turkey, which was dependent on the EC-6. By 1987 the 'Northern Periphery' and the

* France, (West) Germany, Belgium, Netherlands, Luxembourg, Italy.

'European core' had merged, Germany was the pivot for the regional trading system, and parts of the 'Southern Periphery' (notably Spain) had begun to move towards the core. Intraregional trade has grown in western Europe as a whole. Even before the creation of the European Economic Area, the patterns of trade and investment between EFTA and EC member countries were similar to those within the EC. Economic interdependence within the whole region is now very high. By 1991, Germany had become the most important European trading partner for the Visegrad countries, Bulgaria, Romania, Austria, Finland, Sweden, Switzerland and all the members of the EC with the exception of Spain and Ireland.

The development of integrated markets has increased competition among producers, and exposed west European producers to greater international competition. In many sectors there has been restructuring of companies and shedding of overcapacity as companies reposition themselves to compete in larger markets. This process has not always been to the advantage of the Europeans. In the motor industry, for example, Japanese and US multinationals have established strong positions in west European markets, to the disadvantage of nationally based west European firms. In chemicals, a sector in which twelve of the world's twenty largest multinational companies are European, a large increase in the number of mergers and acquisitions within the EC took place in the 1980s.[10] The French government, for example, has encouraged state-owned chemical companies to diversify and internationalize by acquiring a number of companies in both western Europe and the USA. In pharmaceuticals, there has been a particularly strong trend to disperse production across Europe, in order to conform with different national regulations.[11]

Intra-European foreign direct investment has also grown sharply, both in absolute terms and as a percentage of total investment. An intensifying trend of mergers and acquisitions by the 1,000 largest firms in the EC in the 1980s indicates that large companies were seeking to establish a European presence. The counterpart of this trend has been intense competition among countries to attract increasingly mobile firms to invest in their economies. States have therefore come under pressure to adapt national regulations and economic policies to suit the demands of a competitive market.[12]

These trends in the real economy have been closely linked to institutional integration, although the presence for many years of two separate west European trading regimes, in the EC and EFTA, and the weakness of political integration at the level of the OECD, indicate that economic forces alone are not sufficient to explain regional institutional integration.[13] The founders of the EC hoped that integration in one functional area, such as trade, would 'spill over' to integration in others, and indeed this has happened, but the pace was much slower than expected. For many years the main instruments of integration were the customs union, external trade policy and the Common Agricultural Policy, and integration was weak in other areas of economic policy (such as industrial policy, research and development). The Community gradually acquired powers and instruments in new policy areas, such as the Regional Fund in 1975 and the European Monetary System (EMS) in 1979.

In the mid-1980s the integration process took on a new momentum with the launching of the Single Market programme. It was this project which transformed the Community, in the eyes of both domestic populations and those outside. It provided the institutional framework to complement market pressures by creating a single market of 344 million people, or 370 million when the EFTA countries are included. Even though the Single Market remains incomplete (especially with regard to the free movement of people), the creation of an integrated market in an area which accounts for a quarter of world economic output greatly increased the attractiveness of EC membership to other European countries, and convinced significant sectors of the west European electorate, as well as observers outside the region, that (west) European economic integration had become irreversible.

Economic and Monetary Union (EMU) would represent a further considerable step. It encountered more resistance, from both states and public opinion, than the Single Market project, but the EC partners agreed in principle to move towards it in 1989 and worked out the details in the Treaty on European Union agreed at Maastricht in December 1991. Member states agreed to economic convergence towards specific targets in respect of indebtedness, inflation, exchange-rate stability and government borrowing, in preparation for the establishment of a central bank and a single currency (although Denmark and Britain negotiated opt-outs from the third and final stage of currency union). Irrespective of whether all twelve members meet the targets for convergence required for the third stage of EMU, the agreement indicates how far the European states had moved towards accepting a common economic regime. In so doing they recognized that the scope for national management of individual economies had been significantly reduced.

In practice, however, movement towards monetary union faced serious obstacles. In 1991, only three members met the convergence criteria, and it seemed unlikely that sufficient countries could meet the criteria for the third stage to enter into force in 1997. More seriously, strains on the Exchange Rate Mechanism (ERM), which was the basis for economic convergence in the first stage of EMU, jeopardized not only the plans for monetary union but also the stability of the European Monetary System. In the 1980s the EMS had succeeded in its aim of creating a zone of monetary stability in Europe, but in the more difficult conditions of the 1990s, the system became inflexible and fell out of line with underlying economic realities.

As weaker currencies fell to their floor in the ERM, a test of strength developed between central banks and the currency markets, which the central banks were unable to win. First, in September 1992, in the run-up to the French referendum on Maastricht, severe currency speculation knocked Britain and Italy out of the ERM. Then, in July and August 1993, pressure on the French franc and other currencies forced the remaining members to adopt wide bands, which allowed 15 per cent fluctuations around the old parity levels. The underlying cause was the high German deficit after unification, making the Bundesbank unwilling to revise downwards its own interest rates for the benefit of the other members of the system. Economic ministers stated that the wide bands were a temporary measure, and reaffirmed their intentions to proceed with the second stage of economic and monetary union in 1994. However, the agreement constituted a relaxation of the convergence effort, and was a sharp setback to plans for EMU. Afterwards, only the Dutch guilder and the Deutschmark remained tightly linked; an intermediate group of currencies remained in the ERM but floated within wide bands against the mark; and sterling and the lira remained outside. While the EC member states remained formally committed to monetary integration, the events of 1992–3 clearly indicated a swing away from integration.

The stringency of the convergence targets in the Treaty of European Union had raised fears of an EMU-related recession. Under tight monetary conditions, stemming from German unification, the US deficit and other factors, and in the face of weaknesses in the world economy, the European economy declined in growth after 1988 and moved towards recession in 1992–3. A large pool of long-term unemployed grew throughout the EC.[14]

In the past the fortunes of the European Community have tended to wax at times of economic growth and to wane in times of stagnation.[15] The period from 1992–3 was certainly another difficult period for the EC. Nevertheless, the coming of the Single Market and the commitment of governments to sustaining a regime of macroeconomic coordination suggests that west European economic integration is likely to be an enduring trend. But in the short term, the setbacks to institutional integration were serious.

One of the aims of the Community has been to increase the cohesion of its member states and to reduce disparities between regions. Within western Europe, average real GDP per capita tended gradually to converge between 1960 and 1989 among the countries which are now Community members. The ratio of per capita income levels in the four poorest countries to those in the four richest narrowed from 42 per cent in 1960 to 62 per cent in 1989.[16] Disparities within EC member states were reduced in the 1960s and 1970s, then increased in the period of low growth until the mid-1980s, when they again began to fall.[17] Proximity to the European Community certainly benefited the poorer economies of the southern EC members before their accession, although starting from a lower base they had more scope for rapid growth.

A countervailing trend has been strong, for every enlargement of the Community has intensified the distinction between the core and the periphery. The EC-12 remain heterogeneous, with segmented labour markets and different living standards. Large discrepancies persist between the poorest and richest regions, in terms of GDP per capita and unemployment levels.

The Community now finds itself a large rich area with an even larger poor periphery on the outside, stretching from eastern Europe through Turkey and southern Europe to North Africa. Greater political freedom and closer economic relations have increased the salience of economic disparities. One outcome is the increase in migration into Europe, which has grown sharply since the late 1980s. One of the ways in which Europe will define itself will be in the way it responds to this trend.

In economic terms, central and eastern Europe are becoming part of the west European periphery. Having staked their future on the successful transition of their economies towards a west European model, the east European states are in danger of entering a relationship of dependence on the West. The way in which East Germany has been absorbed by West Germany illustrates this danger.

The German economy after unification
German unification is a remarkable case of the attempted merger of two economic systems in one country. As such it may offer pointers to the

larger encounter between capitalist and post-communist economies in Europe. In the speed of the unification and the special circumstances of currency union, however, the German experience has been unique.

German Economic and Monetary Union took place three months before political unification, in July 1990. At a stroke, west German regulations and institutions replaced the east German equivalents. At the same time the Deutschmark replaced the Ostmark, at a parity rate of exchange for private savings (a political decision taken in order to stem the tide of migration into west Germany). This led to a rapid rise in the real wages of east German workers, but at the same time the east German economy suffered an abrupt drop in competitiveness. Most of east German industry was technologically obsolete by west German standards and produced inferior goods which east Germans no longer wanted to buy. Without the former demand for goods from the Soviet Union, and unable to pay wages at the new rate, east Germany's industrial output collapsed, falling by 50 per cent in 1990. The number of people unemployed or on job creation schemes soared to 30 per cent.[18] The Treuhandanstalt, which had been set up to restructure and privatize east German industry, had disposed of a third of the industrial companies by 1992, but was forced to close many down. Despite some spectacular acquisitions, such as those by Volkswagen, Siemens, BASF and others, which took the cream of east German plants, investment was slow to take off. Weak infrastructure, difficulties over property restitution, and the indebtedness and poor environmental standards of east German companies were all obstacles. By 1991 the federal authorities were forced to abandon hope of an economic miracle, and moved towards an interventionist role, allowing the Treuhand and east German Länder to subsidize plants in order to sustain employment.[19] The cost of government transfers to the east rose to over 5 per cent of west German GDP in 1992,[20] with a consequent sharp rise in the federal deficit. This led the Bundesbank to raise interest rates, which had the effect of depressing the German economy and the European economy as a whole. Unemployment in west Germany began to rise, reaching 8 per cent in 1993.[21]

Clearly a period of difficulty was inevitable. With heavy federal assistance the east German economy is likely to recover eventually, and the foundations of the pre-1989 West German economy and political system appeared to be strong. In the short term, however, the post-unification difficulties are weakening the political and social consensus in west Germany and threatening social stability in the east.[22] Whether Germany will be able to maintain intact its successful 'social market' system, based on consensus between companies and unions, at a time of growing pressure on public expenditure, remains to be seen. For some years Germany will be preoccupied with its internal difficulties and will contain a dual economy. Since it will take many years for conditions in most parts of the east to catch up with those in the west, the eastern Länder cannot avoid a position of dependence for some time.

Central and east European trends

In 1945, with the exception of East Germany and Czechoslovakia, the countries of eastern Europe were mainly agricultural, poor, and devastated by war. The communist achievement was to industrialize these economies, with rapid growth rates in the early postwar decades, to raise the level of education, to cut infant mortality sharply, and to provide full employment and social security. But central planning over-concentrated resources in industrial enterprises, failed to stimulate innovation, and offered weak incentives to the working population. Systemic weaknesses, including over-staffing, inefficient use of resources, over-large monopolistic plants, and bottlenecks in the supply system made it more and more difficult to extract growth from the system.[23]

In the 1970s and 1980s, as economic stagnation set in, attempts were made to reform the system, but they met with only partial success owing to political constraints. In Hungary, the reforms of Kadar and his successors decentralized control of the economy to the enterprise managers and introduced some elements of a market economy without politically threatening the ruling elite. Poland's attempt to reform and modernize its capital stock with western loans failed, saddling the country with high debts and an economic and political crisis that the regime could not survive. In the Soviet Union, Gorbachev's reforms also proved costly politically, while actually accelerating the rate of economic decline.[24] In Bulgaria and Romania, Zhivkov and Ceaucescu resisted reforms altogether. The major east European economies thus entered the post-communist period with falling rates of growth and productivity, incomplete reforms, in many cases high debts and deep structural weaknesses. From this starting-point, attempting a rapid transition to a market economy has been a formidable challenge.

As the Russian economist V. Zagashvily has pointed out,[25] a direct transition from a centrally planned to a market economy is not the only nor necessarily the most probable course. A shift from central planning to a system in which state enterprises trade with each other and with the

Table 3.1   Decline of central and east European economies, 1987–92.

	1987	1988	1989	1990	1991	1992 (est.)
Percentage change in GDP						
CSFR	2.1	2.5	1.4	−0.4	−15.9	−8
Hungary	4.1	−0.1	−0.2	−4.0	−10.2	−5
Poland	2.0	4.0	0.2	−11.6	−7.0	−2
Slovenia			−2.7	−3.4	−9.3	−8
Bulgaria	5.4	2.6	−0.3	−11.8	−22.9	−8
Romania	0.8	−0.5	−5.6	−8.4	−13.0	−7
Albania	−0.8	−1.4	9.8	−10.0	−29.9	−11
Estonia	3.1	2.7	3.3	−8.1	−11.0	−25
Latvia	1.5*	6.2*	7.4*	−0.2	−3.5	−30
Lithuania	5.1*	10.7*	1.4*	−5.0*	−13.4	−25
Percentage change in NMP†						
Belarus	n.a.	2	8	−3	−3	−15
Russia	0.7	4.5	1.9	−3.6	−11.0	−20
Ukraine	n.a.	2.3	4.1	−3.4	−9.6	−16
Moldova	n.a.	1.7	8.8	−1.5	−11.9	−30
Armenia	n.a.	−2.6	14.2	−8.5	−11.8	−40
Azerbaijan	4.0	0.6	−0.6	−11.5	−1.9	−30
Georgia	n.a.	5.8	−4.8	−12.4	−25.0	−30

*Percentage change in real NMP
†Net material product

Source: EBRD, *Annual Economic Review 1992*.

world market is another possibility. This transition occurred in some of the reforming economies before 1989, and has taken place in the newly independent republics of the former Soviet Union since 1991. Market economies with authoritarian rule are also possible, as in the case of China. However, transition to an open market economy is essential if the countries of central and eastern Europe are to be integrated into the west European economic system and into the European Community.

Three factors seem most likely to influence the course of market transition: first, the success of the national reform programmes; second, the degree of success in attracting investment; and, third, the proximity and attractiveness of the economy to western markets and to the EC in particular.

'Reform' is a euphemism for a massive process of readjustment, which involves changes in the capital stock, in the sectoral structure of the economy, in the organization of economic institutions and infrastructure, in the tax, banking and legal systems, in the establishment of private property rights, and more broadly in attitudes to economic security and entrepreneurial activity. These changes are bound to take time, and their success depends both on outside support and on domestic public acceptance. Even in the most westernized of the east European countries, reform has proved more difficult than expected.

The collapse of Comecon trade, exposure to world prices and loss of subsidized energy supplies proved to be deep shocks for the east central European economies. Table 3.1 indicates the dimensions of the decline they had entered. While the severity and timing of the crisis varied between countries, all were faced with introducing reform in conditions of deep recession.

Although reforms in Hungary and Poland predated 1989, the new democratic governments in Hungary, Poland and Czechoslovakia introduced new economic reform programmes in 1990, aiming at price liberalization, privatization and stabilization. The Bulgarian and Romanian reforms did not start until 1991, and Gaidar's reforms in Russia only began in 1992.

The Visegrad group were farthest ahead with the reorientation of their economies. In *Hungary*, a stock market, bankruptcy laws, commercial banks and privatization were all made legal before 1989. The government continued reforms at a deliberately gradual pace; political disagreements among the ruling coalition also contributed to unplanned delays. Prices were raised gradually, privatization was confined mainly to small enterprises, and the stabilization programme avoided imposing excessive shocks. The state sector continued to manage 60-70 per cent of industry in late 1992, a figure the government planned to reduce to 30 per cent by 1996.[26] The government retained responsibility for infrastructure and continued to protect agriculture and much of the old welfare system. The cost of this gradualism was a high government deficit and relatively high inflation, but Hungary attracted an inflow of foreign capital. Unemployment rose steadily, reaching 12 per cent by the end of 1992, although it was higher in the east and lower in Budapest and the west of the country. By 1992, although GDP fell by 5–7 per cent, Hungary had much of the institutional infrastructure in place to support a westernized market economy.

In *Poland*, by contrast, the government chose 'shock therapy' in order to deal with the high national debt and inflation running at 30 per cent a month. The Balcerowicz reforms, in consultation with the IMF, involved rapid freeing of prices, tight control of monetary supply, and a sharp reduction in industrial subsidies. The zloty was made convertible and barriers to external trade were lifted, exposing Polish producers suddenly to foreign competition. The government introduced a form of wage control by penal taxation on wage increases. These drastic measures led at first to a steep rise in the inflation rate (to levels of between 500 and 1,000 per cent per annum[27]) in 1990, as previously controlled prices were raised, but by 1991 inflation fell back to about 70 per cent p.a. and to 45 per cent in 1992.[28]

The earlier reforms of the 1980s had partially liberalized foreign trade, banking and the ownership of enterprises. By 1989 a relatively high proportion of the workforce – almost 50 per cent – was employed in the private sector.[29] Balcerowicz's reforms aimed to accelerate the transformation through a programme to privatize both large and small firms. Privatization of the large firms was unsuccessful, since the necessary funds for investment were not available in Poland, and foreign direct investment was low (Poland even became a net exporter of capital in 1991).[30] Small-scale privatization – of shops, restaurants and similar enterprises – proceeded rapidly, however. By 1992 the private sector accounted for almost half of GDP and employed more than half of the population. These were higher proportions than in other east central European countries – though Poland had started from a higher base of private-sector employment.

The economy continued to contract in 1991, but the fall in output stopped in 1992, with a recovery in manufacturing and a positive balance of trade. Unemployment rose to 13.5 per cent by November 1992.[31] The budget deficit grew above limits agreed with the IMF, and this led to the suspension of an agreement on restructuring Poland's foreign debt. The difficulties of the transition contributed to political instability, with three changes of government in 1992. In late 1992 the new government of Hanna Suchocka appeared to succeed in restoring a more stable political climate, and the economy, including industrial output, showed signs of recovery during that year.

While Poland has moved rapidly towards the legal and formal structure of a market economy, it is still a long way from being a flourishing market economy in practice. A stock exchange was created, but shortage of capital has limited its size and activity. Foreign ownership was permitted, but the inflow of foreign direct investment has been disappointing. A strong economic recovery is badly needed to cement in place the reforms which have been achieved.

In the *Czech Republic*, Vaclav Klaus's austere reforms and privatization programme appeared to lay the basis for a rapid transition to a market economy. The Czech Republic had the lowest inflation rate of the central and east European economies in 1992, and unemployment was low despite falling output. Macroeconomic stabilization policies were effective and exports recovered in 1992, although the government balked at implementing tough bankruptcy laws, and enterprises carried a large burden of inter-enterprise debt. In *Slovakia*, where dependence on heavy industry and arms plants meant the withdrawal of subsidies had a much higher social cost, a steep rise in unemployment took place. Disagreements over economic policy contributed to the long political stalemate between Czech and Slovak politicians, which paralysed the federal parliament and led to the economically damaging break-up of the two republics on 1 January 1993.[32]

In these Visegrad countries, reforms were well under way in 1992 and many of the legal and institutional structures of a market economy had been set in place. Trade had been redirected west, and the old centrally planned structures had been dismantled. In all these economies a mixed pattern was developing, with some areas enjoying dynamic growth and others in steep decline. When recovery begins – which is likely to be tied to the recovery of the German economy – these countries, particularly the Czech Republic and Hungary, will be well placed to build on their growth sectors and attract inward investment.

Bulgaria and Romania started their reform programmes later, from less promising initial conditions. Zhivkov's *Bulgaria* had been heavily oriented to trade with the Soviet Union and with the Middle East, and the collapse of this trade hit post-communist Bulgaria hard. The reformed communist party, the Bulgarian Socialist Party (BSP), which won the 1990 elections, introduced price reforms and measures to liberalize the economy, but as economic difficulties intensified, the government was forced to impose rationing and fell in a wave of anti-government demonstrations and strikes. Its successor, the Union of Democratic Forces (UDF) introduced a reform programme in 1991 modelled on those of Poland and Czechoslovakia. This ran into delays because of bitter political infighting between the democrats and the socialists over the pace of the reforms. The unions were also an important political force and were determined to protect the interests of the industrial workers.

A small-scale privatization programme got under way, but (as in Poland) large-scale privatization was ineffective, owing to the lack of capital available for investment. The government therefore continued to

Table 3.2 Exports from central and east European countries to western Europe* in 1928, 1989 and 1991, as a percentage of total exports

Country	1928	1989	1991
Bulgaria	80	21	43
Czechoslovakia	64	34	49
Hungary	63	35	52
Poland	75	41	52
Romania	67	29	40

*Austria, Belgium-Luxembourg, Denmark, Finland, France, Germany, Greece, Italy, Netherlands, Norway, Portugal, Spain, Sweden, Switzerland, UK.

Sources: 1928: Collins and Rodrick, 'Eastern Europe and the Soviet Union in the World Economy', *International Economics*, No. 32, pp. 129–33; 1989 and 1991: International Monetary Fund, *Direction of Trade Statistics*, 1992.

manage state industries, many of which were loss-making. In addition, the government had to struggle with a large debt, and its decision in 1990 to impose a moratorium on repayments meant that Bulgaria was unable to make large new loans. Attempts to control inflation and to reduce the budget deficit also failed. In 1992 inflation ran at about 500 per cent. The budget deficit grew from 8.5 per cent of GDP in 1990 to 10.5 per cent in 1992.[33]

Meanwhile the plunge in industrial output and GDP continued. These difficulties contributed to the fall of the Dimitrov government in late 1992, and its replacement by a government supported by the Bulgarian Socialist Party and the Movement for Rights and Freedoms which planned to increase social and health spending and to accept a target inflation rate of 100 per cent. The lack of significant inward investment, high government indebtedness, slow implementation of reforms and the volatile political situation make it seem unlikely that Bulgaria will emerge quickly from its economic difficulties.

Romania's reforms lagged further behind, and in 1992 falling GDP, inflation of 250 per cent, rising unemployment and declining living standards all pointed to a deteriorating situation. As in Bulgaria, privatization of agriculture proved difficult and politically contentious, and the success of privatization was again limited to the small enterprise sector.

In former *Yugoslavia*, Markovic's attempted reforms failed as the political crisis between the republics deepened. The war devastated the economies of Croatia, Serbia, Montenegro, Bosnia, and Macedonia. Only Slovenia escaped relatively unscathed.

For all the central and east European countries, availability of capital was a constraint on the pace of economic reform. It has been calculated

Table 3.3 Percentage fall in GDP, peak to trough, between 1928 and 1935

Country	Fall in GDP (%)	Country	Fall in GDP (%)
Austria	-22.5	Poland	-20.7
Bulgaria	-12.7	Romania	-5.5
Czechoslovakia	-18.2	UK	-5.8
Germany	-16.1	Yugoslavia	-11.9
Hungary	-11.5		

Source: Angus Maddison, 'Economic Policy and Performance in Europe, 1913–1970', in C.M. Cippola (ed.), *Fontana Economic History of Europe*, vol. 5(2), Fontana, 1976.

that if Bulgaria, the CSFR, eastern Germany, Hungary, Poland and Romania were to begin to achieve the rates of growth met by West Germany in the 1950s and by South Korea since the mid-1960s – doubling income per capita over ten years – they would require an additional $135 billion per year in investment funds. This is equivalent to 15 per cent of annual investment in the EC. At a time of capital scarcity, such sums seem unlikely to be forthcoming. In 1991 foreign direct investment into eastern Europe and the Soviet Union was about $3 billion, of which half went to Hungary. Rollo and Stern calculate that, in an optimistic scenario – in which the countries of eastern Europe and the former Soviet Union stabilize output after falls ranging between 10 and 30 per cent per year and then recover to long-term growth rates of four per cent – capital needs for east European countries would be between three and six per cent of their GNP, which seems too high to be sustained. A pessimistic scenario, which assumes recovery only after 2000 and then growth at two per cent per year, would be compatible with a fairly low level of western investment. The sustainability of high investment is heavily dependent on these countries' prospects for export trade.[34]

The economies closest to the EC were most successful and also found it easiest to restore trade with the West. Some measure of the prewar patterns can be taken from the figures for 1928, for which there are League of Nations data. Table 3.2 compares the exports of central and east European countries in 1928, 1989 and 1991. It shows that in 1991 trade with the West was returning towards the prewar patterns.[35]

In all the central and east European countries, the impact of reforms and liberalization has opened new social and political divisions. It is clear that insecurity has increased and this threatens political stability in some countries. The point at which the economic crisis could overwhelm democratic reform programmes is not easy to predict. In the 1930s, democratic governments in all the central and east European countries except Czechoslovakia fell to authoritarian systems after the crash of 1929. Table 3.3 shows the percentage fall of GDP between peak and trough in a number of European countries between 1928 and 1935. These figures are lower than the drops which have been suffered from 1989 to 1992, although deliberate shedding of production from uneconomic and obsolete plants since 1989 makes direct comparison treacherous.

It is still too early to judge the outcome of the reforms. Much depends on the attitudes of western investors and governments. Despite their problems, the Czech Republic, Hungary, Poland and Slovenia are more advanced in the transition to a market economy. Slovakia, Bulgaria and Romania have further to go. In Russia and the other newly independent republics the transition to market economies faces considerable difficulties.

Russia was the first to launch a programme of radical economic reform, based on Poland's model. This programme, associated with Yeltsin's Finance Minister, Gaidar, aimed to liberalize prices, stabilize the budget and introduce internal convertibility of the rouble. Inside Russia, the immediate effects of price liberalization were to ease the shortages which had become acute in the previous winter, at the cost of increasing inflation. Russia was admitted into the IMF and negotiated a $24 billion package from the G-7 to assist the reforms. Unfortunately the enterprises, many of which were in a monopolistic position, responded to higher prices not by increasing output but by reducing it and raising prices even more. With the enterprises no longer under government control, the volume of inter-enterprise debt built up to unmanageable proportions. The government proved unable to maintain control of its deficit or to slow inflation, which reached hyperinflation levels in 1992. The government was unable to create the preconditions for rouble convertibility, and the international community made available at first only $1 billion of the promised $24 billion package of aid.

The end of the radical phase of the Russian economic reforms was clear when Gaidar fell from power early in 1993, to be replaced by a prime minister representing the party of the enterprise managers. Although a small-scale privatization programme started and market activity developed rapidly (partly emerging out of the former black market, with widespread mafia operations), the bulk of the economy remained in state hands. A new tax system proved incapable of raising taxes on a large scale. Banking remained rudimentary, so that most people held money in cash form. Governments clearly feared the consequences of closing loss-making enterprises, and for the time being they preferred the alternative of inflation, and continued economic isolation as a result of the non-convertibility of the rouble.

The *Baltic states* had been among the richest republics of the former Soviet Union, and their secession improved their relative situation. Their currencies appreciated strongly vis-à-vis the rouble, even though they remained weak relative to western hard currencies. However, they suffered economically from the sudden break with Russia and from the sharp loss of former trade. Latvia, for example, experienced a fall in output of some 40 per cent in 1992, and had no work for the mainly military plants in the cities. The political conflict with Russia threatens the traditional transit trade. Trade with their Scandinavian neighbours offered important opportunities, but the Baltic states need to find a new basis for their economies if they are to become, as they hope, regional Hong Kongs.

The European Community and eastern Europe

The European Community is in a position to dominate the wider European economy, since it accounts for over 80 per cent of GNP in the area up to the borders of the former Soviet Union. The EC has been able to dictate the terms of the Europe agreements, and in these and the other agreements to establish a wider free trade area, market regulation, competition policy and environmental policy will have to be brought into line with EC standards.

The position of the east European countries is more unfavourable than that of the Mediterranean group at the time of their accession. Like the Mediterranean countries, they have emerged from a period of authoritarian rule, and need access to the Community to underpin their domestic stability. However, the changes required to turn their economies into flourishing market economies are more profound and they start from a deep recession. If they can follow the same process of 'catching up' that the Mediterranean countries experienced after 1960, they have much to gain from trade with the EC. But this will require considerable changes in their institutional infrastructure and the willingness of west European economies to provide market access and investment.

In relation to both eastern Europe and the world economy, the EC faces a choice of directions. On one course (Fortress Europe) it could become a more closed bloc representing west European interests. In such a structure, strong lobbies would seek to resist reform of the protectionist agricultural policy and avoid enlargement to the east, as well as calling for a defensive stance in world economic fora. On another course (Fragmented Europe) individual states might become protectionist and enlargement would not take place. A third course (Wider Europe) would be to open the Community to east European states, compromising some of its short-term interests in order to develop its interdependence with its eastern neighbours and its world partners. This course would imply willingness to accept the accession of the east European states, while giving interim assistance to make accession possible. In the long term the benefits of this course for the Community would lie in the contribution that eastern Europe could make to the European economy. In the short term, however, the avoidance or mitigation of potential instability is more important, since failure of the transition is likely to have costly implications in political and security terms. There is much that could be done to assist the transition: revising the Europe agreements; investing in infrastructure (communications, transport, etc.); supporting the introduction of better banking services and new legal frameworks; assisting with training and education. Private investment, professional dialogue, and social and educational exchanges are also important.

Whether the Community is generous or not, the east Europeans have little choice but to accept EC trade on whatever terms they can get, and they will have to accept the Community *acquis*. The Community seems likely to benefit from a large free trade area in eastern Europe. Both the Wider Europe and the Fortress Europe scenarios could therefore lead to strengthened economic relations between both parts of the continent; whether this relationship develops into an unequal hegemony or a more balanced partnership will depend on how policy is made in the coming years.

4

NATION, STATE, UNION: CHANGING PATTERNS OF GOVERNANCE

Integration and disintegration have been twin themes of post-Cold War Europe. In 1989–90, the decision of the EC member states to advance towards European Political Union suggested a move beyond the nation-state just at the time when the collapse of the Soviet bloc had led to the re-establishment of autonomous nation-states in eastern Europe. By 1991–2, a strong nationalist reaction was running as opposition developed in western Europe to the proposed European Union, and national minorities challenged newly established states in the east. These turbulent cross-currents reflected the strength of both unifying and dividing forces in Europe, which are influencing the prospects for west European integration and the political outcome of the east European reforms.

Unifying and dividing forces
The modern states of western Europe developed at a time when communications within states were bad, social and economic conditions were immensely varied, most people rarely travelled far from their birthplace, and people knew little of life outside their own country. Now European societies are complex and mobile; living conditions, especially in cities, have become homogeneous; instant communications and rapid mass transport have made most of the continent accessible. Motorways, air travel, railways, faxes, television, and other common products of a technological society have brought about closer contact and created a superficially common cosmopolitan culture. Yet Europe retains its nations, its cultural diversity, and its distinct political systems.

The strongest unifiers are those of technological standardization and economic development. As Chapter 3 has shown, the sustained growth of the European economy after 1945 created a densely interconnected west European market, with similar products, forms of production and economic relationships. Transnational companies created a demand for similar qualifications and working practices across states, and came to use plants, workforces and contractors distributed across state boundaries. The internationalization of capital flows, similarly, has transcended national divisions. The formation of the Single Market is a stimulus to convergence in national standards and social policy, and to fiscal and legal harmonization; and the creation of the European Economic Area and the extension of the customs union to eastern Europe through association and cooperation agreements will extend these unifying pressures to the wider Europe.

The experience of 45 years of peace, prosperity and free movement between societies has also brought about a degree of convergence in political systems and social attitudes among west European societies. Parties such as Christian Democrats, Social Democrats and Liberals have sustained common ideologies and patterns of conflict over many years.[1]

Similar issues have come to connect the different national debates. More than anything, the Europe-wide debate over European Union indicates the linkages between domestic politics in different countries. The development of the European Parliament and European lobbies such as the European Trade Union Confederation and the Union of Industries of the EC is a sign of a new level in the west European polity, even though these bodies are still weak compared with their national equivalents.

These economic, social and political processes build on a strong sense of shared culture in western Europe, despite the cleavages between North and South, Protestant and Catholic. Large-scale intra-regional movements of people within Europe are also significant. Around 150 million tourists travel across borders within western Europe every year[2] and although some no doubt cause divisions rather than unify, these large flows, together with student exchanges, business visits and foreign workers, have created a more open and multinational continent.

The unifying forces are reflected in a high level of public support in EC member states for 'efforts being made to unify western Europe'; according to a Eurobarometer poll in 1991, 80 per cent of respondents were in favour of such efforts.[3]

Nevertheless, the majority of people in western Europe do not *feel* European, but rather identify themselves mainly with national or sub-national groups. While there has been an important development of multiple identities in slightly less than half the population in EC countries, virtually half of the population still say that they never feel European. In response to a Eurobarometer survey asking 'As well as feeling (your nationality), how European do you feel?', 49 per cent of respondents in the EC replied 'Never', 33 per cent 'Sometimes', and only 15 per cent 'Often'. Elite groups, however, have a much stronger sense of west European identity; indeed, a cleavage has developed in many European societies between those who through their business or personal inclinations think in European terms and those who have a more nationalistic consciousness.

Nations remain of vital importance as sources of identity and as linguistic and cultural units. Distinct from states and from peoples,[4] they are the main repositories of history, collective memory and myth.[5] The west European model of the nation has been based on the identification of the citizens with a particular territory, and on their shared identity and history, and usually a shared aspiration to take their own decisions.[6] Where a single state has been built on more than one nation, as in the British Isles and Spain, the dominant nation rules the state, though not without a long history of strife and accommodation with the other nations.[7]

The coming of nationalism and liberalism in the eighteenth and nineteenth centuries was the most important change to the European system of states before globalization and regional integration. By making the state the mouthpiece and arm of the nation, nationalism created a new entity, the nation-state, which had a new basis of legitimacy in national self-determination. Nationalism spread unevenly, affecting France from 1789, the central European states from 1848, Italy with the *Risorgimento* of 1870, and Poland, Hungary and the Balkans in the late nineteenth century. The Paris peace settlements of 1919 were the high point for self-determination, and by 1945 the nation had become the basis for the international order, according to the Charter of the United Nations, which rhetorically declared itself a 'free association of nations'.[8] The effects of nationalism on the order of states were to include the legitimation of force in national interests and the creation of powerful contradictions between the principles of self-determination and sovereignty. The association of sovereignty with nationalism created a fragmented order which harnessed the passions and energy of the masses to the interests of the state. The explosive tensions which the nation-state system could generate, and not contain, were fully evident in the first half of the twentieth century.

The achievement of modern nationalism was to weld the nation to the state, but the fit between nations and states was often imperfect, especially in eastern Europe. Until the nineteenth century, central Europe, eastern Europe and the Balkans were dominated by multinational empires. When they disintegrated at the end of the First World War, the territorial settlements left many peoples of the region divided between several states. Consequently the process of nation-state formation took place later than in western Europe, and was intrinsically more difficult given the distribution of peoples. This was to be a serious weakness of the post-Cold War order, when the new east European democracies returned to the model of the western nation-state.

The nation, and nationalism, are fundamental to political systems in both parts of Europe; but they play different roles. In western Europe, the political classes combine a sense of national self-interest with acceptance of European political integration. Nationalism, in the sense of vigorous identification with the home nation, is strong, but exclusive nationalism has been mainly limited to political movements outside the political consensus.

In eastern Europe, however, nationalism was a powerful force, with strong support in governments and political parties. Long-suppressed nations at last had the opportunity to express their national identity and national culture. Ukrainians, for example, perceive their nationalism as a positive and unifying force. Having experienced the liquidation of their intelligentsia in the 1930s, and the destruction of much of their culture under communism, they were only now engaging in the process of nation-building which was completed in most parts of western Europe in the nineteenth century.

Other forces too are fuelling nationalism in post-communist societies. Insecurity and powerlessness fed a popular appetite for simple solutions and strong leaders. In some societies, former communists were able to maintain themselves in power by riding the nationalist wave; in others, nationalism was associated with a wave of anti-communism. Once under way, exclusive nationalism generated counter-nationalism, and has contributed to insecurity and fragmentation.

Trends in governance in western Europe

The west European state is squeezed between these two sets of forces. States which can no longer control their own economies or defend themselves alone are obliged to join institutions and regimes in order to carry out policies effectively.[9] But nations remain the main focus of identity. This has opened a gap in western Europe between what people feel to be their political community, and the transnational and intergovernmental level at which economic policy, security planning, and other policies are increasingly determined.

The state has become, in a sense, both too big and too small. It is too big for small nations trapped inside larger states, like the Scots or the Catalans; it is too small for those who would like to see stronger governance at the European level. For those who hope for a new transnational European political culture based on cities, regions, or other levels of aggregation, it is the wrong institution altogether.[10]

The state in western Europe is tending to share more and more of its functions with other states.[11] Defence passed out of the independent control of states and into the management of alliances with the formation of NATO. The regulation of trade has passed to multilateral institutions such as GATT and the EC. Law-making has become shared between member states and the EC. The Single Market has also induced most states to coordinate their social and immigration policies and control of their borders. Few areas of formerly domestic policy have been untouched. The pressures for convergence also apply to states outside the EC; even Cyprus, for example, routinely enacts many EC directives within its own domestic legislation.[12] Small states have always been exposed to the behaviour of their larger neighbours, but now all states are losing elements of their sovereignty.

States began to become porous, granting some powers to international organizations, and others to local governments and regions; and this was one way to ease the tension between the nation and the state. However, the pattern varied greatly. The federal states, Germany, Austria, and Switzerland, already had local governments with significant powers and could in principle adapt themselves readily to upward and downward delegation of powers. Italy's regional governments took on an enhanced role in the 1970s, enabling public authorities to provide services which central government could not deliver. Democratic Spain eased national tensions by its willingness to cede powers both to Brussels and to its regions. Belgium attempted to accommodate its discontented nations, though with only partial success, by granting the Fleming, Walloon and German-speaking areas a considerable degree of self-government. Even centralized France embarked on a programme of devolving financial and executive powers to elected regional governments in the 1980s; Corsica in particular gained a special degree of autonomy. The trend was for the emergence of a 'meso' level of governance in Europe, at the level of the region (in Belgium, France, Italy, Portugal, Spain), the Länder (in Germany) or the county (in Norway, Sweden and Denmark).[13] This was linked to a growing consciousness of the regional level, expressed in the aspiration for a 'Europe of the regions'. The concept had the virtue of flexibility, since it allowed for a level of cooperation below the state level and for different kinds of relationships between different actors. Thus Bavaria could express its independent tendency by emphasizing its regional policy; Slovakia could develop relationships with comparably-sized regions.[14] Cities, too, were linking up across Europe, as were citizens' movements. These were forms of 'bottom-up' integration which offered an alternative to 'top-down' integration by the states. Unitary Britain resisted the trend and strengthened central powers at the expense of local government during the period from 1979, despite strong demands for greater autonomy for Scotland.

Above the level of the state, what has emerged in the EC is not a replacement of state power, but an additional layer of governance – one created by states and managed by them. The European Coal and Steel Community and the customs union were attempts to regulate areas of conflict between states, and thus to improve the effectiveness of governments in these sectors by coordinating their policies. Similarly, EC member governments have attempted to coordinate their foreign policies since 1970. The process has been described as a fusing of state powers.[15]

Despite the pressures on it, the nation-state remains the firm focus of political life and political cultures. Party politics in Europe are still overwhelmingly national, and the need for political leaders to win support from national electorates clearly constrains the development of a European political system. Cross-national parties have yet to develop (with the possible exception of the Greens), although attempts at policy coordination between parties sharing similar platforms in different countries have increased; the existence of the European Parliament creates an incentive for coordination.

Radical change is difficult to secure in established party systems, yet they have proved adaptable to change. Lipset and Rokkan argued that national political systems, because of their inertia, tend to be anachronistically structured: 'the party systems of the 1960s reflect, with few but significant exceptions, the cleavage structures of the 1920s ... the party alternatives, and in remarkably many cases the party organizations, are older than the majority of the national electorates.'[16] This might suggest that the mould of national politics will be slow to break. However, old political parties have been prepared to take on new agendas and to abandon earlier ideologies. The well-established pattern of right–left polarization between Christian Democrats (or Conservatives) and Social Democrats, with smaller Liberal parties, remained the dominant European pattern, although the original basis for these parties waned as religious and trade union affiliations weakened, and as the service sector grew at the expense of the industrial and rural sectors. The communist parties became marginalized after the 1980s, while new political forces emerged in the form of the Greens and the radical right-wing parties.

Even before the end of the Cold War, many west European party systems were experiencing a phase of growing volatility,[17] measured by movement of voters between parties between elections, change in the distribution of voters along the 'left–right' axis and changes in the number of parties with parliamentary representation. The position of the parties also seems fluid as societies adjust to new conditions, including those resulting from globalization and European integration. The debate over the Treaty on European Union appears to have opened a new pattern of polarization at a time when the old patterns were particularly fluid.

Although the idea of a 'United States of Europe' was current in the immediate aftermath of the Second World War, the project of political union – as opposed to economic union – has been hard to establish. Proposals for steps towards political integration in the 1970s and 1980s failed to muster agreement, and it was not until the Single European Act (1985) that member states agreed (not without sharp controversy) 'to transform relations as a whole among their States into European Union'. Disagreements about the ultimate shape of the Community continued up to and through the negotiations which led to the Treaty on European Union. The states which wanted to move towards a federal Europe with a stronger supranational element (the original EC-6 together with Spain, Portugal and Ireland) could not convince those (Britain and Denmark) which preferred to emphasize intergovernmental cooperation. The Treaty on European Union was therefore a compromise. Its three-pillar structure extended the areas of economic policy under supranational control while strengthening intergovernmental mechanisms for foreign policy and home policy. It created an embryo of political union, but left considerable power with the states; and it was the European Council and the Council of Ministers with its network of committees, rather than the Commission or the Parliament, which remained the primary policy-making bodies. The European Community was therefore far from becoming a super-state, yet it was considerably more than a regime, for not only did its member states agree to adopt common policies in key areas of state policy, but they had also created transgovernmental structures and supranational institutions capable of coordinating and giving effect to their decisions.

However, the wide-ranging treaty, with its explicit objective of moving towards a common defence and a common currency, drew a sharp public response in western Europe. On 2 June 1992, the Danish citizens shocked the European governments by narrowly voting to reject the ratification of the treaty. Their rejection threw the new treaty into question, since its implementation depended on the ratification of all twelve signatories. On 26 June 1992, the Council of Minsters met in Lisbon to consider their response. It was clear that the Danish referendum would force a tactical retreat from Maastricht. The governments emphasized the principle of subsidiarity, according to which

> the Union shall only act to carry out those tasks which may be
> undertaken more effectively in common than by the Member States
> acting separately, in particular those whose action requires action by
> the Union because their dimension or effects extend beyond
> national frontiers.

This opened the possibility of a redefinition of how far individual member states were committed to full participation and some clawing back of powers by the states. But because subsidiarity is a bottom-up principle, it also implies powers being exercised at levels below the state. The Lisbon summit also discussed linking the European Parliament more closely to national parliaments and striking a new balance between the Community, the national states and the regions.

For the first time, the future of the European Community became a common political issue in western Europe, and the Danish rejection, followed by the very narrow French 'yes' in September 1992 and a close debate in the British parliament, led to a year of uncertainty which further weakened the prospects of an early federal or politically integrated western Europe.

The debate over the Union coincided with a wave of change which began to sweep across west European political systems, in part as a ramification of the end of the Cold War. In Italy, for example, the 45-year-old pattern of polarization between the left and the right broke up, with the joint share of the Christian Democrats and the Communist Party falling from 73 per cent of the vote in 1976 to 46 per cent in 1993. The

Figure 4.1 The extreme right in Europe: electoral performance in 1991/2

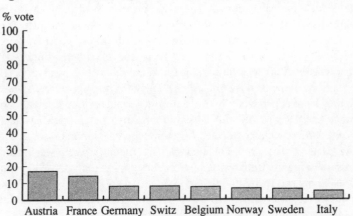

Key: FP – Freedom Party, FN – Front National, DVU – Die Deutsche Volksunion, Rep – Die Republikaner, SD – Schweizer Demokraten, APS – Schweizer Auto Partei, VB – Vlaams Blok, FN – Front National, PP – Progress Party, ND – Ny demokrati, MSI – Movimento Sociale Italiano–Destra Nazionale.
Source: Research and Analysis Department, FCO.

regional political forces such as the Northern Leagues developed strongly, benefiting from a strong tide in favour of political reform. This opened the way to a restructuring of the party system, an attack on corruption, and a greater transfer of powers to the regions. In France, the weakening of socialism led to a landslide victory for the Gaullist right in the 1993 elections, which followed the divisive campaign over the Maastricht referendum in 1992. The referendum campaign had pitted the political establishment against nationalist reaction and opened a divide between those who appeared to be beneficiaries of the European integration process (the towns, the professionals and the more prosperous regions) and those who felt threatened (farmers, the unemployed, people in areas of uncompetitive industry and those with fears of immigration). In Denmark those who voted 'no' in June 1992 included two-thirds of the unskilled workers and 60 per cent of workers in the public sector, as well as fishermen opposed to EC fishing policy, farmers opposed to the reforms of the CAP, older voters who could remember the Second World War, and nationalists concerned about immigration. In Britain, the European issue created deep divisions within both the major political parties; the split within the governing Conservative party was unusually long and public.

There were also signs of a growth in right-wing nationalism in a number of European countries. The recession and dissatisfaction with the political system were important factors. This movement was often expressed as hostility to immigrants, and led to attacks on 'guest-workers' and asylum-seekers in Germany, Austria and elsewhere. Figure 4.1 shows the level of electoral support for right-wing nationalism in 1991–2. These movements were not strong enough to gain power in any state, but they were capable of winning power in certain regions (southeastern France and parts of Austria). More importantly, they influenced mainstream parties, which competed for their support by moving some way towards their platforms. For example, EC member states were under pressure to impose tight restrictions on immigration in response to popular reactions and fears of violence.

West European nationalism can be seen as a response to insecurity and the threats to national and even personal identity from the sweeping changes that more open west European societies were experiencing. In 1992–3 the momentum towards integration was still strong, but the potentially fragmenting effects of nationalism and parochialism offered a growing threat to it.

For smaller countries, like Denmark, the Nordic countries and Switzerland, the issue of participation in the Union opened divisions between potential beneficiaries and potential losers, as well as playing on the fears of small nations about control of their own destinies.

Nevertheless, the basic pattern of western constitutional liberal democracy was very strongly established, and there has been a trend for countries on the periphery of the EC to converge towards it. Spain and Portugal moved towards a west European style of democratic system following the removal of their military governments. In the Spanish case, the system of proportional representation was copied from Belgium, at the suggestion of Maurice Faure, then rapporteur of the European Parliament.[18] There were also economic pressures which pushed political systems in a similar direction, for example in influencing the size of welfare systems. This has been especially striking in the Nordic countries. In Sweden and Finland, new coalitions came to power in 1991 intent on reducing welfare expenditure and improving economic performance to achieve greater competitiveness in the European market. The Swedish model of neutrality, extensive social welfare and social democracy, which had offered a distinctive alternative to the dominant patterns inside the former blocs, appeared to be eroding under this pressure.

Despite the diversity of west European political systems, the commitment to a common pattern of liberal democracy provided a basis, in compatible institutions and values, for closer integration. What remained uncertain was whether, having built a limited degree of political integration on the basis of cooperation among elites, sufficient mass support existed to carry it further.

In summary, the west European pattern remains one of fragmentation between national political cultures, but increasing integration between states. The unifying forces appear too strong for a return to a *Europe des patries*, but the dividing forces are also sufficiently well established to make a strongly integrated European federation with a common political culture unlikely in the near future. The changes in west European political systems since 1990 make it entirely possible that the progress of integration could be checked, and even reversed. It is possible to imagine the trend continuing towards different circles of integration and cooperation in different policy areas, a process that is already established, if understated.

The weakening of the nation-state in western Europe appears to be compatible with the development of closer political cooperation across European states, and yet a state-like structure at the European level appears to be incompatible with national political diversity. If Deutsch's notion of a pluralistic security community is taken as a reasonable model for the European order, an intermediate course, to avoid the dangers of a return to fragmentation, would be to develop the unique qualities of the EC as a community of societies, capable of building multiple levels of governance on the basis of multiple identities, while avoiding the creation of a United States of Europe.

Germany

The changes in the German political system following unification offer a particularly interesting test of the feasibility of integrating an ex-communist society into a western democratic political system. German political developments will also have an especially strong bearing on the prospects for west European integration or fragmentation. It therefore seems worth examining the particular circumstances of Germany in more detail.

Having regarded itself from 1945 to 1989 as one nation divided between two states, Germany found itself after 1989 as one state, with two rather distinct national identities.

Few people [writes John Ardagh] had any special desire to retain a 'GDR identity': yet they felt deeply coloured by a common experience that marked them off from West Germans; and as they entered a new highly competitive world, they even felt fearful of losing some of the slow, gentle, compassionate values that had been bred of having to survive under the old regime.[19]

In 1984 only 42 per cent of West Germans thought of Germany as one nation,[20] and the tensions that emerged between 'Wessis' and 'Ossis' over jobs and financial transfers set limits to the extent of a shared national identity.

The very stable postwar political system in West Germany had been based on economic prosperity, good industrial relations, and a constitution which produced stable coalitions, consensus and continuity. The proportional representation system, with its five per cent hurdle, deprived extremist parties of a political base, and the distribution of powers between the federal government, the Bundestag, the Bundesrat and the Länder encouraged consensual decision-making. The postwar generation's rejection of militarism and nationalism helped to shape West Germany's character as a mainly civilian and trading power. West Germans followed Thomas Mann in preferring a European Germany to a German Europe, and Germany became one of the most enthusiastic protagonists of the European Community. Although fears and doubts about the dangers of a new German nationalism were never entirely extinguished, even amongst chancellors and former chancellors, postwar West Germany was a stable society committed to the active construction of a peaceful European order.

In the aftermath of unification, a surprisingly rapid convergence occurred in political attitudes. In 1990, when it became clear that unification would take place, the east German opposition movement New Forum splintered and parties corresponding to the west German parties dominated the elections for the Volkskammer in March 1990. By the time of the all-German elections in December of that year, voting patterns in both west and east Germany had become remarkably similar. Opinion polls indicated convergent political attitudes and values on a wide range of issues.[21]

Democratic institutions were established very quickly in the five new Länder, by the simple expedient of unification under Article 23 of the Basic Law (which stated that 'other parts of Germany' could accede to the Federal Republic). Over 4,000 west German civil servants were placed with the eastern Länder,[22] to bring their administration into line with west German standards, and to replace personnel who had been compromised by association with the *Stasi*. The east Germans were therefore expected to adjust wholly to the west German system, and no attempt was made to adapt the federal system to the new circumstances.

Nevertheless the addition of five new Länder and 10 million new voters was bound to affect the federal system. The addition of the new Länder changed the existing political balance among the Länder and between the Länder and the federal government. The five new Länder were dependent on the federal government, and were therefore in no strong position to bargain. Moreover, the size of the financial transfers to the east were so large that the financial autonomy of the eleven old Länder, especially the poorer ones, was threatened. Björn Engholm, the Minister-President of Schleswig-Holstein, warned that these developments could lead to a decline in German federalism.[23] Meanwhile the development of right-wing extremism in the new Länder indicated the political dangers of the high level of unemployment and social insecurity there.

In 1990 the writer Günter Grass warned passionately of the dangers of German unification, and argued for a confederation instead.[24] It is possible that the 'takeover' model of German unification, combined with the relative lack of sympathy and integration within German society, may be storing trouble for the future. It is clearly not enough to extend western regimes to the societies of the former eastern Europe: much deeper contacts between societies and peoples are necessary to reintegrate the former blocs.

Because of Germany's central position, its political stability is a linchpin for stability in the wider Europe. It is too soon to judge the long-term domestic effects of unification, but there is little doubt that, in the short term, both the political and the economic stability of the Federal Republic have suffered.

The political transformation of central and eastern Europe
In the former eastern Europe the balance between unifying and dividing forces is very different. Globalizing forces, of the kind which have become such important phenomena in western market societies, began to penetrate only weakly before the 1980s. While they were important as an agent of change by opening gaps between centrally planned and market societies, their influence is not as deep and has different effects in these

societies. The east European post-communist societies strongly rejected old forms of quasi-integration. The successive collapse of Comecon, the Warsaw Pact and the Soviet Union destroyed the main institutions for international and inter-republican cohesion. The intended and unintended effects of their removal left east European states on their own outside any strong transnational regimes. The newly independent republics of the former Soviet Union have responded to crises in one another's economies by seeking to cut their links, although they were so interdependent that this was not immediately possible. The central and east European states were determined to escape from their former trading and security relationships, without immediately being able to join western economic and security regimes.

In most post-communist societies, the state is very weak, compromised in the eyes of the citizens by the experience of the communist years. Tax bases are poor, government debts are high, the enforcement of law and order is feeble, and the state's authority is limited even in state-managed sectors. This is compounded by political confusion and economic crisis. In the former Soviet Union, the situation is particularly difficult, for there distances are so large that regions tend to fragment naturally in the absence of effective political coordination.

Where the state is weak and civil societies poorly developed, national identities are often the only significant basis of collective identity. For many, the reality of the post-communist experience has been one of falling living standards, and sharply rising insecurity. At a time of turbulent change and social uncertainty, it is not surprising that people feel a need to identify with groups capable of offering them a sense of identity and security. In many formerly communist societies, intermediate forms of social association, above the level of the family, have been destroyed or weakened by communist rule (with the exception of the Church). In the countries of the former east European bloc and the newly independent republics, the nation was already a focus for resistance to the communist regimes. Nationalism has therefore been capable of mobilizing broad popular support. It takes two forms, one apparently healthy – identification with the national group and celebration of national culture – and one more dangerous – exclusive nationalism which is capable of promoting one nation at the expense of others. Here, as in western Europe, the two forms have common roots and often tend to merge into one.

This combination of weak and divided states, and powerful nationalism, is especially volatile in eastern Europe because of the very poor fit between nations and states. The weakness of group rights and of human rights in general encourages minority nations to aspire to statehood. Where states lack legitimacy, secession movements can succeed; and the struggle for power that ensues in such situations readily engenders violence.

The revolutions of 1989 were committed to introducing civic societies, human rights and democratic systems, modelled on the democratic political systems of the West. But it was difficult to impose these new values from above. The reformers were trying to cultivate the flower of democracy not only in the acid topsoil of post-communist societies, but also on the subsoil of older historical and cultural traditions, which continued to exert a powerful and subtle influence.[25]

These traditions differed in each society, and a general analysis of political trends throughout the region is therefore difficult. Nevertheless it is possible to identify some general patterns in the process of transition away from communism and to distinguish factors which help to explain the divergent courses these states are taking.

A useful starting-point is the 1920s, which offer many parallels to the post-Cold War situation. The newly established states in the region all had a turbulent political history in the interwar period. Czechoslovakia was the most successful case of a constitutional democracy, and despite tensions between Masaryk's vision of a Czechoslovak state and the aspirations of the German and Slovak minorities, the new state and its democratic character survived intact until its overthrow by Hitler in 1938. Poland re-emerged with a well-established national culture which had survived the period of Russian rule and laid the basis for a state which Polish leaders and their western allies saw as a bulwark of the east central European order and a counterweight to both Germany and Russia. Domestically, however, the struggle for power between fourteen parties in the *Sejm* produced thirteen coalition governments between 1919 and 1926, when Marshal Pilsudski established his dictatorship. The Baltic states, too, experienced a bewildering succession of coalitions, though parliamentary rule survived until the early 1930s. In Hungary the large landowners dominated politics from the brief episode of communist government under Bela Kun to the fascist period. In Yugoslavia (before 1929 the Kingdom of Serbs, Croats and Slovenes), rivalry between the Serb governments and Croat opposition dominated politics. In Albania tribal structures were the basis of rule.

Common to most of these states (except Czechoslovakia) was a low level of modernization. Peasants were the largest social group, landowners remained important, and the middle classes were small. Political parties tended to be coteries of friends rather than expressions of social interest groups. The political elites and bureaucracy held power with relatively weak accountability, and informal influence and patronage were important, despite formal systems of constitutional rule.[26] Most of these states also had significant problems with national minorities. In the Baltic states, for example, despite exemplary legislation for minorities during the 1920s, tensions developed with the Baltic Germans in the 1930s which were to prove a critical weakness.[27] Further south, Serbia settled Slav peasants in Kosovo and forced half a million ethnic Albanians to emigrate from the region. In some respects, the course of events since 1989 has been more a return to indigenous patterns of political development than a return to (western) Europe.

The upheavals, traumas and suffering of the Second World War continued after its end in eastern Europe, as communist regimes established their power and crushed resistance. In due course they built a new domestic order, based on a great expansion in the role of the state and the new division of society into the 'nomenklatura' and the industrial and agro-industrial workforce. By introducing similar economic and political conditions, the communist regimes imposed a degree of uniformity on eastern Europe, although in every case the political system became a hybrid of communist regime with earlier historical forms. In Bulgaria, for example, the communist regime which came to power in 1944 achieved a remarkable reshaping of society.[28] It turned an agricultural country into a primarily industrial one; it created a much larger industrial proletariat than had existed before; it destroyed the social power and wealth of the middle class; and out of a nation of small peasant farm holdings it created the largest agro-industrial complexes in Europe outside the Soviet Union. In the towns the regime demolished middle class family housing and built new blocks of flats. All this required a swollen bureaucracy, which became the new governing class. The regime controlled all public associations and used the secret police, backed by concentration camps, to suppress opposition. Eighty-six camps held 200,000 people, out of a population of less than nine million.[29] This hardline regime survived until 10 November 1989.

Other communist societies had already begun to reform before 1989. The political transformation was most advanced in Hungary. By the mid-1980s, the reforms of the Kadar regime had clearly failed.[30] Central planning had been relaxed, but a new power structure based on coalitions of factory managers, regional party bosses and the industrial ministries was thwarting attempts to introduce market disciplines to the economy. Real wages were falling, and many Hungarians became dependent on second and third jobs in the 'black' or 'shadow' economy. An open split between reformers and hard-liners developed within the Communist Party, after Kadar dropped the reformers from his government. By 1988 the reformers had come out on top.

Now committed to both economic and political reforms, the regime conceded relaxation of censorship in 1988, and prepared legislation allowing freedom of speech, freedom of assembly, an independent judiciary, and the election of non-communist deputies to parliament. In 1989 the Communist Party, suffering a rapid fall in membership, calculated that its best hope of survival was to form a coalition with other parties and fight free elections. After round-table talks with the new political parties, the government amended the constitution in September 1989, to make Hungary a democracy, to introduce elections, to create a presidency, and to abolish the Communist Party's leading role in the state. The elections took place in March 1990 and produced a victory for the opposition party, the Hungarian Democratic Forum (HDF). This gradual transition process ensured a peaceful and stable change of regime.

The communist regimes in eastern Europe were doomed from 1985, when Gorbachev had decided on the so-called 'Sinatra doctrine'.[31] But it was some time before either the regimes or the people appreciated this. In Poland (where the unions and the Church were a well-organized focus of opposition) and in Hungary, decisions to hold free elections had been taken before November 1989. The regimes in East Germany and Czechoslovakia fell quickly and were replaced by democratic governments. The Baltic states, too, experienced large demonstrations of 'people power', and largely avoided the crushing Soviet response that many had feared. In Bulgaria, the reforming communists, in the renamed Bulgarian Socialist Party, won the 1990 elections and remained in power until October 1991 when the 'dark blue' (radical conservative) wing of the UDF democratic coalition came to power. In Romania, the National Salvation Front and its successor the Democratic National Salvation Front held power in coalition with other parties, in a volatile political situation marked by growing nationalism. In Yugoslavia, nationalist former communist politicians won the first free elections in 1990, starting a process of national polarization which led to war in 1991. In Albania, a communist government remained in power until 1992, when the Democratic Party won the elections.

In the first phase of the transition from communist rule, the dissent movements which had been prominent in the revolutions of 1989 took a leading role. Figures like Lech Walesa, Vaclav Havel and Arpad Goncz became presidents of the new states. 'Return to Europe' was one of the themes of the revolutions, and in the prevailing euphoria leaders upheld the aspiration of a rapid move towards democracy and the development of civil society and full human rights. In time, however, the ambiguities of what a return to Europe meant were to become politically important.

The political systems which developed during this early phase were notable for the very large number of parties which emerged from the disintegration of the umbrella popular movements such as Civic Forum and Solidarity. They were also characterized by presidents with powerful personalities, although varying amounts of real power (contrast Zhelev, Walesa and Goncz). Great importance was attached to the Constitutional Courts which often played significant roles in disputes in the new democracies, for example in Hungary over the respective rights of the president and the prime minister to dismiss the heads of the state-owned radio and television.

Gradually the number of parties dwindled and professional politicians began to take over from the charismatic leaders of the dissent period. In Hungary, for example, although eighty parties contested the March 1990 elections, only six took seats in parliament after obtaining the constitutional minimum of 4 per cent of votes cast. The two largest parties, the HDF and the Alliance of Free Democrats (AFD), defined their aspirations in European terms. Both agreed on joining the EC and NATO, on adopting a market framework, and on seeking European standards for minorities. They differed in that the AFD, a more cosmopolitan party, urged a rapid transition to a market economy, while the HDF favoured a gradual approach, and was more nationalist and ruralist. The HDF defined itself as a party based on the ideals of conservative Christian democracy, national liberalism and populist nationalism; its aim was to find a road to Europe which preserved the traditions, values and national consciousness of Hungarians, both in Hungary and abroad. The AFD defined itself in terms of European and Hungarian liberalism, emphasizing human rights and civil liberties, and the restraint of state power.

Nevertheless, Hungary's statist political traditions retain a strong influence. Public attitudes are coloured by a belief that the state can solve all problems, and a tendency to collectivism which has its roots in a pre-communist, semi-modern society.[32] Nor had the political culture broken away from some aspects of the communist past, in particular an expectation that governance would come from the top down, and a view that the way to bring about change is to have friends in powerful positions. Despite the transition to democracy, Hungarians remain used to patron–client relationships, and the public sector remains a 'spoils society'.[33] In part this reflects the growth of the black economy and of corruption during the later period of the communist regime, but it also goes back to older Hungarian traditions.

Similarly, in Bulgaria all political parties claimed to support the introduction of a market economy and multi-party democracy and sought entry into the European Community. Yet the problems of economic and political transition tended to concentrate minds on the divisions of the past before the future could be addressed. This was a critical issue in the debate over privatization and property restitution, which were essential for the transition to a market economy. The Union of Democratic Forces (with a political base mainly in the large towns) aimed to restore conditions to those which had prevailed before the communist regime, even if this meant restoring land to owners who had been dispossessed for 40 years; the Bulgarian Socialist Party (which had come to represent primarily the interests of the farm-workers) argued for transferring ownership of factories and cooperative farms to those working in them. Since the large agro-industrial complexes were created by amalgamating many small plots, the privatization process opened real social conflicts between the former owners and people who had become dependent for their livelihood on arrangements created since the communist seizure of power.

The development of new social cleavages such as these was an important feature of the post-communist transition. Income differentials began to open sharply, with a small but wealthy middle class emerging from the ranks of the former *nomenklatura* and enterprise managers. Other groups, such as pensioners and workers in loss-making state factories, suffered sharp falls in living standards. In Hungary, for example, half the population suffered a decline in real income and a fifth saw a sharp increase in their income between 1989 and spring 1991.[34] A large middle class, of the kind which forms the stable basis of social mobility in northwest European societies, did not exist. Nor did political parties yet correspond closely with social interests.

After the initial decisions to create a market and a democratic system, the development of market economies and the political transition proceeded separately, with their own dynamics. Power struggles and disputes over the treatment of former communists preoccupied parties, and this inhibited close control over the development of the economy. In

Hungary, for example, politicians spent much of 1992 worrying about the survival of the governing coalition, after the split in the Independent Smallholders Party and the opening of rifts in the ruling Hungarian Democratic Forum;[35] meanwhile parliament was unable to carry out crucial reforms in the state budget and in the welfare system. As Chapter 3 has shown, the state still retained control of important parts of the economy, and so political paralysis had a serious impact. In most countries, including Hungary, the banking sector remained primarily under state control, and channelled private investment into supporting state-owned enterprises instead of new domestic private investment. Nevertheless, the market was creating sizeable groups dependent on its existence, with a strong interest in maintaining it; this dynamic was particularly clear in Poland, the Czech Republic and Hungary but it was evident in other east European countries too. The market system thus had a self-sustaining dynamic, despite the volatility of democratic politics.

By 1992–3 the combination of constant political crisis and sharp deterioration of the economy was having a strongly negative impact on public perceptions of the reform process. Disillusion set in. Turnout in elections in Hungary and Poland was disappointingly low. Polls carried out by Eurobarometer in east European countries and former Soviet republics in autumn 1992 showed that most respondents in the entire region (51 per cent) thought that their country was going in the wrong direction; only 31 per cent thought it was right. Poles and Hungarians were more pessimistic in this regard than people in the Ukraine and European Russia, though in the Czech Republic and Slovenia a majority felt that their country was going in the right direction. In most cases majorities of respondents were dissatisfied with the development of democracy in their country. Lithuania was the only country in which more were satisfied than dissatisfied. Support for joining the European Community was strong throughout the region (ranging from 92 per cent in favour in Slovenia to 70 per cent in favour in European Russia). However, asked how often they think of themselves not only in terms of their own national or ethnic identity but also as European, only a twelfth 'often' see themselves as European, 24 per cent 'sometimes' and 61 per cent 'never'. European identities were higher in countries remote from western Europe than in the Visegrad countries (see Figure 4.2).[36]

The disillusion was deepened by a recognition, among both policy-makers and publics, that the 'western values' to which the democratic revolutions aspired were not necessarily those practised even by western countries. Despite its declarations of support for openness and free trade,

Figure 4.2 Frequency of thinking oneself European

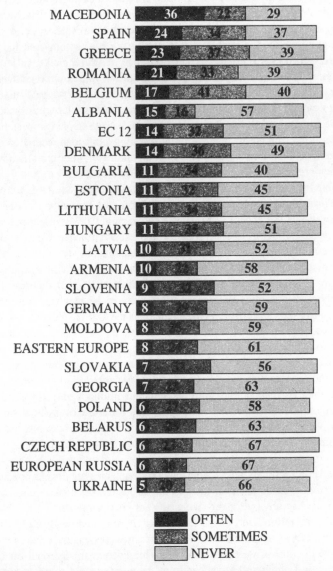

The figure shows responses to the question: 'Do you ever think of yourself as not only (nationality) but also a European? Does this happen often, sometimes, never?'

Sources: Central and East Eurobarometer, no. 3, 1992; *Eurobarometer* 37, 1992.

in practice the EC was perceived to discriminate against east European products and to hold east European societies at a distance.[37] Similarly its policy in Yugoslavia was perceived as failing to sustain European values. Therefore, despite almost universal agreement on the broad principles of market economies, democracy and stability, actual as opposed to declared values in western and eastern Europe were perceived to differ.[38]

Those who championed these 'all-European' values were gradually losing political ground. Havel was marginalized by the particularist forces which brought about the unwanted split of Czechoslovakia; Zhelev in Bulgaria and Goncz in Hungary both struggled to sustain a moderate line on issues like de-communization and social reconciliation in political situations where confrontation and radical conservatism had the upper hand.

The growth of nationalism throughout eastern (and western) Europe also threatened the prospects for a liberal view of a wider Europe in which the values espoused by Havel, Goncz and Zhelev might prevail. The main political project in central and eastern Europe after the disintegration of the Soviet bloc was the re-establishment of independent nation-states. This was to revive a form which was difficult to apply in eastern Europe because of the mixed distribution of nationalities. The problem of minorities became a serious flaw in the new east European state system, with terrible consequences in the former Yugoslavia and clear dangers in the Baltic states, Slovakia, Greece, Macedonia, Kosovo, Bulgaria, Romania and the former Soviet republics. The basic weaknesses in practice of civic society – the tendency to associate citizenship with national groups instead of with the whole population in a state, and the weak traditions of human rights, let alone minority protection – held the potential for serious conflicts. The rising influence of nationalism, in response to economic uncertainty and insecurity, as expressed by populist nationalist leaders throughout the region, was a sign of the dangers of returning to a 'fragmented Europe'.

Despite these divisive tendencies, nationalism was developing in a different environment from that of the 1920s. In the 1990s competing great powers are no longer rivals in western Europe and do not have irredentist designs on eastern Europe as Germany and Italy had in the 1930s. Moreover, the movement of information, people and goods across relatively open borders was modifying the context for nationalism and the nation-state. This was apparent in the development of cross-border cooperation in eastern as well as western Europe, which led to the formation of so-called 'Euro-regions'. For example, Hungary, Poland,

Slovakia and Ukraine signed an agreement to set up a Carpathian Euro-region in February 1993, with the support of the Council of Europe, aimed at improving communications and contacts between communities and peoples divided by the borders in this region. Similar developments are under way in the Neisse Euro-region between Poland, the Czech Republic and eastern Germany, and the Oder Euro-region between northwestern Poland, eastern Germany and southern Sweden and Denmark. Polish and Ukrainian officials have considered establishing a similar region along their common frontier.

These initiatives represent a step towards reducing the divisiveness of borders and can be a positive contribution to minority problems. Nationalist politicians in Poland have criticized the Euroregions as suggesting a new partition of Poland, yet the development of these regions appears to have a 'bottom-up' momentum of its own.[39] Other less benevolent transnational trends can also be noted, including the development of cross-border crime on a large scale in eastern Europe, and the developing phenomenon of 'diaspora nationalism'.

While the establishment of nation-states is a strong trend, elements of a 'multi-level' society have been developing in eastern as well as western Europe. Outside international institutions play a very important role, especially the IMF. The influence of cross-national social movements, news media and market pressures has also grown – the nation-state in eastern Europe has become more porous, especially since 1989.

It is clear that the model of a 'return to Europe', on the basis of west European models and values, is an inadequate framework for assessing the process of political transformation. It ignores the multiplicity of west European models, the importance of historical traditions, and the differences between espoused and practised values. Distinctions can be drawn between societies with political traditions closer to western Europe, with political systems which seem compatible with western democracies, and those where democracy is not yet well-established, where authoritarian traditions are strong. But the more fundamental trend may be a return to indigenous political traditions.

Conclusion

The traditions of the wider Europe are of three broad areas in which different forms of governance have prevailed.[40] The historical west European tradition has been one of open governance, separation of powers, towns and Church with some autonomy from the state, the rule of law, and competition for authority between different institutions. The east European tradition (especially in Russia) has been one of strong government, few intermediate institutions between the ruler and the ruled, and a weak or non-existent civil society. Central Europe has been intermediate between these two traditions. There has been a tendency for western models and ideas to diffuse eastwards, but usually with a lag, and usually with distortion.

If one speculates that these historical patterns will reassert themselves, then the new Europe could be seen as again developing three broad zones (not necessarily geographical ones).[41] In the first, the density of connections between societies has led to the formation of strong transgovernmental and transnational links, which are modifying the traditional state system and at the same time mitigating the strength of traditional nationalism. The nation-state system remains, and some post-1989 trends are encouraging fragmentation, but the trends towards convergence, especially those driven by the formation of a large open trading area, are strong. In the second zone, the nation-state is being re-established, and nationalism is very powerful, but the international and supranational organizations present in the first zone have a strong influence, and there are pressures to make a political transition towards polities that are compatible with those in that zone, even if these societies remain distinct in political character and economic performance for many years. The third zone would contain those states or regions which are overcome by political and economic crises, and take on authoritarian forms of government.

The post-Cold War period has brought an altered pattern of governance throughout Europe, and fundamental changes in the relations between states, societies and international organizations. On the one hand, the old paradigm of west European integration carried through by elites without much public debate appears to have reached a natural limit; on the other, the nation-state structure can no longer effectively manage the challenges of governance in western and eastern Europe. Elements of a new order can be detected in the development of European regions, in the domestic influence of international organizations and regimes, and in the growth of transnational and transgovernmental links. European patterns of governance seem likely to remain heterogeneous, and unlikely to support a strong Fortress Europe, and yet the patterns of political development in western Europe seem too similar to lead to a newly Fragmented Europe, at least in the West. A wider Europe based on close political integration is not a practical possibility, but there do not yet appear to be fundamental barriers in respect of systems of governance to a looser European grouping including at least the western and central and some of the east European societies; indeed, transgovernmental and transnational links between these societies have begun to emerge.

Nationalism, either when it is allied to the power of a state and pitted against other states, or when it confronts the government of a state under the control of another nation, is potentially a force of enormous destructiveness. Its re-emergence is a worrying feature of the post-Cold War order. Yet nationhood is also a fundamental and enduring aspect of collective identity. The linkage between the nation and the state is still strong in Europe, but the forces of globalization are weakening it; the ultimate destiny of the nation does not have to be the control of its own state. Nations can find expression in multinational contexts, including in the construction of transnational cultures and polities, and it is not necessary for self-determination to be expressed in the creation of new states.[42] As Seton-Watson concluded in his study *Nations and States*, 'there must be a balance between national cultures and international cooperation … if destructive civil wars and nuclear holocausts are to be avoided.'[43] The development of such a balance is one of the critical tasks in the construction of a new European order.

5

FROM COLD WAR TO HOT CONFLICTS: THE CHANGING INTERNATIONAL ORDER IN EUROPE

The end of the Cold War at first offered the prospect of a Europe unified and freed from divisions. But it gradually became clear that Europe was still divided, not into two halves, but into several regions at different stages of development. Parts of western Europe had reached a phase of social and economic development in which the requirements of governance had outgrown the nation-state. Parts of eastern Europe, in contrast, were in a phase of new state-building. The Balkans had returned to an anarchic state system reminiscent of the early twentieth century. The newly independent republics of the Soviet Union formed a special group, halfway between a suzerain state system and an independent state system. Hungary, Czechoslovakia, Poland and Bulgaria found themselves in an intermediate position between the multilateral system to their west and the fragmenting state systems to their east. The breakdown of the Cold War structure thus produced in Europe a new system of international relations of considerable complexity.

It is commonplace to describe what has happened as the replacement of a bipolar by a multipolar system. In many respects this explanation does illuminate events. In so far as nation-states are still crucial actors in the international system, the development of a multipolar system (a trend which preceded 1989 by about 20 years) and the abrupt end of bipolarity in 1989–91 were critical changes. However, changes in the structure of

Nationalities and conflicts in central and eastern Europe

Figures show the percentage of the largest national group in total population

✳ Armed conflict since 1989

the state system have affected the applicability of the concept of polarity. Is the EC a pole in the international system, or are its member states poles? Can the concept of polarity apply to different levels in the international system? To the extent that the international society is becoming a multi-level system in Europe, the polarity paradigm breaks down.

Globally, the main realignment in international relations has been from a bipolar system to a core–periphery structure. The world system can now be seen in terms of a 'core' group around the OECD, with the triad of the USA, Japan and the EC at its centre; an inner periphery of industrialized but less economically advanced states; and an outer periphery of developing countries. The core dominates the world economy, controls the major world capital flows and enjoys the highest per capita incomes. Relations between countries in the core and periphery are ambivalent: on the one hand, societies in the periphery seek to join the core, on the other, they resist the core's hegemonic tendencies.[1]

This change of alignment is especially clear in Europe. West European societies form part of the international 'core', which sets the rules of the main international institutions and regimes (GATT, IMF, G-7, EC, etc.). The opening of eastern Europe to the world economy increased the importance of these institutions there, although the populations in the region had little access to participation in their decision-making.

The core–periphery perspective must be qualified, however, by the complexity of relationships among the states of the periphery. The end of the bipolar system has led not only to new relationships between western and eastern Europe, but also to new patterns of international relations within western, central and eastern Europe. The loosening of Cold War ties in both parts of the Continent has led to a much more fluid system of international relations.

Moreover, a general reordering of policy areas is under way. Until near the end of the Cold War period, military and nuclear issues dominated relations between the blocs while trade and other issues were managed mainly within them. In the immediate aftermath of the Cold War, military issues between the major powers became less salient, while interdependence grew in trade, migration and other issues between eastern and western Europe. Western markets became crucial for east European economies after they reoriented much of their trade westwards, but east central and east European economies are of great potential significance for western Europe too, especially in sectors such as agriculture and steel, in which they are capable of producing large supplies of highly competitive products.[2] The numbers of people on the move between the eastern and western parts of Europe and between different parts of central and eastern Europe are increasing rapidly.[3] The sending and receiving countries are interdependent because economic conditions and government policies in both sets of countries influence the scale of migration, and both groups feel its political and economic effects.[4]

In the security field, the Yugoslav crisis demonstrated how new national conflicts could reverberate in the security policies of both eastern and western Europe. Since these policy areas were linked both to each other and to policies in several states, it was difficult to frame a response to events in one policy area (such as migration) without taking steps in others (such as aid, trade or investment policy). In these respects, the problems of the wider Europe were becoming common problems, which required a common response.

None of the institutions and regimes which emerged out of the Cold War period were structured to manage these all-European issues. Indeed, the end of the Cold War appeared to leave a large empty space in the European 'architecture' of institutions, as though the building site had suddenly expanded after the buildings for it had been constructed. Some of the western institutions began to colonize the space in the eastern part of the site, and new east European associations were set up for regional cooperation. Policy-makers approved the notion of a 'complementary and interlocking' structure of existing institutions, but there was no disguising the fact that some of these would have to change to fit the new circumstances.

Meanwhile a kind of vernacular architecture was also springing up, in the form of transnational contacts between societies. Television and advertising transmitted western cultural and social influences, while contacts between peoples, businesses, and non-governmental organizations proliferated in the period before and especially after the end of the Cold War. Such inter-societal contacts affect the foreign policy priorities of governments, by shaping citizens' expectations of the direction in which their countries are moving, and through their influence on domestic politics. This was particularly clear during the popular revolutions of 1989–90, when the dissident groups, steeped in transnational contacts, came to power in eastern Europe.[5]

The development of international institutions and transnational contacts is balanced, however, by the fragmentation brought about by the creation of new states in eastern Europe and the resurgence of nationalism. The interaction between these opposing forces is likely to shape the prospects for conflict and cooperation in the post-Cold War years.

1989 as a settlement

The European settlements of 1919 and 1945 both contained within them the seeds of future conflict. The changes of 1989 produced in effect a new postwar peace settlement, and initial hopes for the new order were very high. The German President, Richard von Weizsäcker, for example, referred to 'a pan-European historical process, which has as its aim the freedom of the people and a new peace order in our continent',[6] and the CSCE Charter of Paris looked forward to 'a new era of democracy, peace and unity'.[7] The declaration by NATO and Warsaw Pact members that they were no longer adversaries set the seal on 45 years of military confrontation.[8]

Although there was no formal peace conference to end the Cold War, the 'two-plus-four' talks between East and West Germany and the Four Powers, the bilateral Soviet–German treaty and the German–Polish treaty provided a legal basis for the settlement of the German question. By the standards of previous postwar settlements,[9] that of 1989–90 can be judged positively. It was a legitimate settlement, peacefully arrived at, which created no states with an interest in overthrowing it; it brought to an end a long period of conflict without creating a new one; and the former adversaries reaffirmed CSCE principles, which laid a framework of norms for managing future conflict between them. The Europe of 1989 was therefore a hopeful one.

By 1991, however, the prospects for stability did not look nearly so good. The break-up of the Soviet Union and Yugoslavia, taking place in circumstances of minimal legitimacy, in effect produced a second reshaping of Europe. In the post-1991 order, at least two states had potential grievances over their situation in the new state system – Russia, because of the 25 million Russians beyond its borders, and Serbia, with 2 million Serbs living in other republics of former Yugoslavia.

Before 1989, it seemed that nuclear deterrence had brought to an end the era of war-fighting between great powers. States with nuclear weapons could no longer use force against one another for political purposes without mutual destruction. Policy-makers in both blocs regarded the system of mutual deterrence, buttressed by clearly defined borders, as a highly stable system.[10]

After 1989, it seemed that Europe had slipped into three overlapping security systems. In most of western Europe, including the neutral countries of EFTA, there existed a security community in which war did not seem credible, despite the absence of an external threat. Between NATO and the CIS, a security regime still operated, based on deterrence, arms control and confidence-building measures. In eastern Europe there was a security vacuum. Previously frozen internal conflicts flared up again and by 1991 war-fighting (though not between great powers) had returned in the Balkans and in peripheral parts of the former Soviet Union.

Despite the new sources of instability, the central feature of the new European security system was the diminution of external threats between the large powers. This was reflected in the striking arms control agreements after 1989. In October 1991 NATO's Nuclear Planning Group approved the withdrawal of 80 per cent of the US nuclear weapons deployed in Europe;[11] in June 1992 Presidents Bush and Yeltsin signed an agreement to reduce the number of strategic warheads in their arsenals from 10,000 to 3,500 on each side by 2003. New confidence-building measures were also agreed. In March 1992 the Open Skies agreement permitted all NATO members, five former east European Warsaw Pact members and Russia, Ukraine, Belarus and Georgia to fly observation flights over one another's territories.[12] The Conventional Forces in Europe (CFE) Treaty signed in November 1990 for the first time restricted to agreed limits the number of personnel, tanks, combat aircraft, artillery pieces and helicopters in the armed forces of all European states. The republics of the former Soviet Union agreed to apportion the quotas of treaty-limited equipment amongst themselves by a joint declaration signed at Tashkent in May 1992. These treaties included provisions for intrusive verification, thus constituting a significant limitation of national sovereignty in an area in which sovereignty had been considered inviolable.

In addition to these military agreements, all the European states, including the new ones, together with the republics of the former Soviet Union, the United States and Canada, agreed to abide by CSCE agreements, which effectively codified the rules and norms of the 'international society' in the wider Europe. These rules included the ten principles of the Helsinki Final Act of 1975, affirming respect for the sovereign rights of states, the obligation to refrain from the threat or use of force, the inviolability of borders (which were not to be changed except by international agreement), respect for the territorial integrity of states, the obligation to settle disputes peacefully, non-intervention in internal affairs, respect for human rights, the equal rights and self-determination of peoples, cooperation among states, and fulfilment of obligations under international law. To this core the CSCE gradually added new standards, some of which have further limited the absolute degree of state sovereignty. For example, it has been accepted that the observation of human rights and the treatment of minorities by member states are not solely internal matters, but matters of legitimate concern to all CSCE members. CSCE standards, together with those of the UN Charter and the provisions of international law, had come to represent the declared principles of the European international order. They protected the rights not only of states but also of individuals and national groups.

The CSCE also developed new machinery for regular international consultation in crises, through the Committee of Senior Officials of CSCE member states, a Conflict Prevention Centre for the exchange of military information, and new procedures for invoking inspection missions in the event of complaints about abuses of CSCE standards.[13] Since the CSCE operated on a consensus principle, its ability to enforce policies was limited to what could be mutually agreed, and other European institutions were stronger in relation to their member states. Nevertheless, the CSCE's norms were an advance on previous standards and were accepted by all the states of Europe.

Other European institutions and regimes are considered below, but first it is worth considering the significance for the European order of the central event of 1989.

German unification

The fall of the Berlin Wall rendered obsolete the enormous military concentrations in central Germany, led to the toppling of the east European regimes, and set in motion a stormy process of accelerated development in the European Community. It also led to the unification of Germany, an event with profound consequences for Europe. Would Germany remain the same kind of partner in western regimes, or would it become a hegemon, or even a superpower in central Europe?

Before unification, West Germany's economic might was not translated into military strength or national power projection. It was common to see Germany as an 'economic giant and a political dwarf'.[14] It took a secondary role to the USA in NATO, and by no means a dominant political role in the EC. The emphasis of German foreign policy was on coalition and consensus-building, through both *Westpolitik* and *Ostpolitik*. *Deutschlandpolitik*, the aim of eventual unification, was seen as a very long-term policy. Chancellor Kohl said in 1988 that he hardly expected to see a united Germany in his lifetime.[15]

The policy of Foreign Minister Hans-Dietrich Genscher had been one which gave weight to the 'new complexity of world politics',[16] and which regarded economic strength and bargaining power as the basis for Germany's foreign policy. Policy would be exercised by shaping relations of complex interdependence.

This policy was applied in the approach to German unification. Genscher said, 'We seek the process of German unification in the context of EC integration, the CSCE process, East–West partnership for stability, the construction of the common European house and the creation of a pan-European peaceful order. We Germans do not want to go it alone or to follow a separate path. We want to take the European path.'[17]

Chancellor Kohl's emphasis was different, but he too saw the future of Germany within the context of a stronger EC which could play a larger role on the world stage: 'Only a unified EC can mould the future of this continent and take on responsibility in the world together with the United States'.[18] In the words of his colleague, Alfred Dregger, western Europe was to 'stride out'[19] into world politics led by a strong Federal Republic. But the CDU party to which they belonged also acknowledged that Germany was constrained by interdependence. As the largest exporting nation in the world, with a lack of natural resources, its interests could not be fulfilled at a national level. German security and international stability were interdependent: 'We have our own interest in political, economic and social stability around the world, in tension-free relations with all states and in open secure routes around the globe.'[20] Therefore the German government would aim to protect its national interests through supranational and international means.

The achievement of unification was not a planned outcome of German foreign policy, but the consequence of popular movements in East Germany. Kohl's first reaction to events was his ten-point plan of 28 November 1989, which called for a confederal structure between the two Germanies, only later leading to unification. When it became clear that the East Germans were intent on unification, Kohl dropped the ten-point plan and instead proceeded to rapid unification of the East German Länder under Article 23 of the Basic Law. It was the need to stem the flow of emigration into West Germany which led first to the economic and monetary union, in July 1990, and then to political union in October 1990.

The basic force driving events came from the people, and politicians in other countries recognized that there was little they could do to check them. However, as the diplomatic community began to respond, German politicians made efforts to acknowledge the interests of their partners in the process.

The agreement of the Four Powers was necessary to give legal approval and to settle the future of the NATO and Warsaw Pact forces in the two Germanies. The two-plus-four talks provided the framework for these negotiations, in which the German government knew it had to win the approval of its partner governments for a sustainable succession. The Soviet government accepted the inevitability of German unification in December 1989, but the issue of alliance membership was to prove a stumbling-block for six months of difficult negotiations. Gorbachev at first insisted on either German neutrality, or German membership of both NATO and the Warsaw Pact. Eventually in July 1990 he dropped his opposition, in exchange for a package of financial and technical assistance; at the same time the NATO summit of 5–6 July eased the way by adopting in its London declaration a statement of non-aggression between the pacts. The agreement that Germany could stay in NATO, provided that only German troops without nuclear weapons were to be deployed in east Germany, was a substantial Soviet concession.

The German government was also keen to maintain the support of its EC partners and accepted the French view that closer European integration was necessary to cement the larger Germany into the EC. Federal ministries discussed the process of unification in detail with their counterparts in other EC member states and with the European Commission. Thus, while it was clear that German unification would go ahead in any case, there was a collective wish to place unification within the framework of western regimes, including the EC and NATO. The European Council of 8 December 1989 stated that German unification 'must come about by peaceful and democratic means, respecting all treaties and agreements as well as the numerous principles on dialogue set out in the Helsinki Final Act. It must also be embedded within the framework of European integration.'[21]

Incorporating the East German Länder into the FRG meant an EC 'enlargement without accession';[22] in this case, however, the negotiations took only five weeks.[23] The European Council, at a special meeting in Dublin in April 1990, agreed that unification could go ahead without modifying the EC treaty. West German and EC law were to apply in east Germany, although it was clear that it was far from complying with many of the EC rules and standards. Germany's interest in rapid unification combined with the convenience to the EC of avoiding special accession arrangements for a separate state. The initiative and momentum clearly came from Germany; nevertheless, the EC dimension of unification was an important additional element. The European Parliament commented that unification was 'the greatest and in its form the most unique historical experience which contributes to the dismantling of barriers between eastern and western Europe and to the realization of the wider goal of European Union'.[24]

In seeking to use the opportunity of rapid unification, the German government acknowledged the importance of multilateral consultations. State treaties and the formal approval of Germany's partners legitimated this key event shaping the new order.

The end of the Cold War restored Germany to its central political position in the continent. In economic terms, west Germany already had a central role. But by absorbing east Germany, a unique state came into being that straddled the division between capitalist and post-communist systems and inherited the links of the former East Germany with eastern Europe. East German foreign policy disappeared completely, being taken over by the west German Foreign Ministry.

Hans-Dietrich Genscher declared 'We Germans will not forget that our position in the heart of Europe has placed us not *between* West and East but in the centre of Europe – as a part of the *one* Europe.'[25] This suggested that *Ostpolitik* would remain a vital element in German foreign policy, especially since Germany, among the western societies, was most exposed to instability in the east.

Germany also had a central position in the network of European institutions. As the largest European state, playing a central role in NATO (unlike France), in the EC (unlike Britain), in the transatlantic relationship, and in the relationship with central and eastern Europe, Germany was in a position that gave it considerable influence and power. It was through regimes, rather than as a nation-state, that it wielded influence.

Investments by German corporations in Czechoslovakia, Hungary and Poland exceeded those of other countries, and German corporations attempted to buy up the best assets in the Czech lands and east Germany. But this should be interpreted as an outcome of a capitalist system penetrating an economically distressed post-communist one. There is no evidence of a German foreign policy aim to establish national hegemony or dominance in central Europe. Unlike in the early twentieth century and the 1920s, Germany in the 1990s is a satisfied state, both in economic and in foreign policy terms.

Although it is the largest economy in the Community, Germany nevertheless has remained dependent on the EC economy. In 1991, 54 per cent of west German exports went to the EC, and a further 16 per cent to EFTA countries, so that altogether western Europe accounted for

70 per cent of west German exports. For the German government, participation in regional integration structures has been a means to influence the main trading areas and hence a vital interest.[26]

Simply by virtue of its size and wealth, Germany exerts a strong influence on its neighbours. They are more likely to adopt the rules and procedures that govern the most successful economy than others. The first two articles of the treaty on Monetary, Economic and Social Union specified that the model for east Germany would be the social market economy. This model was also influential elsewhere in eastern Europe, and Russia decided to adopt it in principle. The federal system provided a powerful model which the German government wished to promote for the development of the European Union: a federal Europe with strong regions would fit relatively easily around the German system. Similarly, because of its economic weight, the Bundesbank became the model for the proposed European Central Bank.

Size, centrality and importance in regimes were already giving Germany a growing role in Europe, and adding weight to German foreign policy objectives. Until the 1970s, German foreign policy conformed closely to US policies, but subsequently Bonn took a more independent line, for example, over the Yom Kippur war, *Ostpolitik*, the Siberian gas pipeline and the modernization of short-range missiles. The EC became a convenient vehicle for Germany to express a foreign policy that began to diverge from the US position. In the period up to 1989, Germany's policies of *Westpolitik* and *Ostpolitik* were decisively influencing the European order, while US foreign policy, which had contained the Soviet Union and Germany through NATO, came to lag behind priorities and realities created in Germany.[27]

Yet the shadow of the past and constitutional limitations made it difficult for Germany to play a leading role. The proposal to change the constitution to permit German forces to fight abroad raised impassioned debate. Germany was a strong protagonist of a powerful Common Foreign and Security Policy (CFSP) for the EC, precisely because this would enable Germany to avoid the implications of a national foreign policy and defence.

Chancellor Kohl's foreign policy adviser, Horst Teltschik, argued that Germany's new role would be not as a dominant power, but as a weighty influence in regimes:

> Just as the Federal Republic of Germany in the past was no political dwarf, so will united Germany not be a 'world power'. But it can be seen even today that this Germany is taking on new weight and new

quality in international politics ... For us Germans, the question does not arise whether we are or want to be a 'world power', but how we are in future to handle our newly acquired weight responsibly ... The ideological confrontation is giving way to competition between systems and rules of political, economic and cultural action ... All these perspectives of European integration and pan-European umbrella structures leave no leeway for great-power or world power policy by a united Germany. What they instead call for is energetic and creative pursuit by German policy of a new European architecture within which we shall be ever less sovereign but ever more an integrated component of a community. That is how the new Germany will find its identity in Europe.[28]

This policy is dependent on two conditions: first, the survival of the institutions and, second, the insulation of Germany's political system from extremist nationalism. In 1992 the German population was influenced by doubts about political and economic aspects of the European Union project,[29] by fears about the loss of the Deutschmark, and by rising nationalism, although extreme nationalists remained a marginal group. The political class was clear about the choice facing Germany. Chancellor Kohl said in June 1992: 'If we don't link German unification with European unity, if what we undertook in Maastricht fails and we don't achieve European Union in the last decade of this terrible century, then we will revert to nationalist disputes in Europe next century.'[30] The former foreign minister Genscher expressed the same fears: 'It's a question of whether we forge ahead with European union or descend into nationalistic egotism now that the Soviet Union is dissolved and the threat of its dominance eliminated.'[31]

The European Community

The immediate effect of German unification was thus to spur a further phase of integration by the European Community. The Maastricht Treaty was the result of two parallel lines of development, on Economic and Monetary Union, and on the Political Union itself. The first followed on from the Single European Act, beginning in June 1988 when the Hanover European Council called for the Commission and the governors of central banks to prepare the ground. The Delors report on the subject was published in April 1989, and the Rome European Council of October 1990 accepted the proposals for a single currency and a European Central Bank.[32]

The second line developed more abruptly following German unification. Chancellor Kohl and President Mitterrand agreed to bind the new Germany to a strengthened European Community: 'In view of the profound transformations of Europe, of the establishment of an internal market, and of the achievement of economic and monetary union, we think it is necessary to accelerate the political construction of a 12-member Europe.'[33] Accordingly they wrote to their EC partners in April 1990, proposing an Intergovernmental Conference (IGC) on Political Union.[34] They urged reinforcing the EC's democratic controls, to legitimize a political union, making EC institutions more effective, ensuring economic, monetary and political cohesion, and establishing a CFSP. The extraordinary meeting of the European Council in Dublin on 28 April set in motion a process for an IGC on political union and another on economic and monetary union in late 1990.[35]

The debate that ensued was about the future shape of western Europe. Germany was not the only country whose position in Europe was changed by the end of the Cold War. While the Continent was divided, France had occupied a central and initially a leading position in western Europe and in the EC. Through the EC, in which the Franco-German relationship was central, French policy-makers felt able to contain Germany and to play an equal political role. The new wider Europe would be one in which the role of France would be less prominent, and potentially, one in which the Franco-German relationship might be put under threat.[36] Britain, too, faced a radical change in its policy environment. The special relationship with the USA, which played a critical role in maintaining Britain's defence capacity, and its 'bridgehead' role between America and Europe, had lost its strategic significance; in April 1989 President Bush was alarming British policy-makers by speaking of a 'partnership' between the United States and Germany.[37] Margaret Thatcher's Atlanticism and strident opposition to the EC was a stand against the tide of events. Britain and France at first resisted rapid German unification, but both bowed to the inevitable.

It was a debate conducted, at this stage, between states and their governments. The French government's vision for Europe – an integrated western Europe, including a common foreign and defence policy – fitted the postwar French aim of developing a foreign policy independent of the United States.[38] Instead of an enlarged Community, President Mitterrand proposed a European confederation, with a strengthened Community at its heart:

My *grand projet* is ... to turn the whole of Europe into one space
... a single and vast market ... This is why I have talked about a
confederation ... I would like to see a strong nucleus capable of
making political decisions effectively. This is the Community.
Within the Community and Europe, I would like to see France – we
are working at it, and it is not easy – become a model of economic
development and social cohesion. That is my plan.[39]

The German government, too, had a vision of a Europe based on its
own national model. This implied a federation of states with effective
and democratically accountable federal institutions. It also wanted to
increase the policy scope of the EC as a regime, by bringing foreign and
security issues, home and justice affairs into the Treaty of Rome.

The Länder exerted an independent influence in the negotiations.
Their representatives met Jacques Delors, President of the Commission,
in May 1988, to explain their concern that future integration should not
reduce their role in relation to Bonn and Brussels; the emphasis on
subsidiarity was in part a response to this demand.[40] The Committee of
the Regions was seen as a first step towards empowering the regions in
EC affairs.

In the case of Britain, the personal battle that developed between Mrs
Thatcher and Jacques Delors had the effect of pitting Britain against the
other eleven member states. This was to lead to Mrs Thatcher's fall in
December 1990, but even afterwards the British posture was scarcely
communautaire. The main issue for the British negotiators was the clash
between an intergovernmental and a supranational Community. The
British government strongly opposed substantial transfers of sovereignty
to the Community and aimed to set limits to the powers of the EC
institutions. The British negotiators resisted the mention of a 'federal'
vocation in the Treaty of Union, and opposed bringing foreign, security
and home policy into the scope of the Rome Treaty.

The shape of the European Union which emerged from the negotiations was inevitably a compromise. The Treaty proposed significant
increases in the supranational powers of the EC in economic policy,
while leaving the coordination of foreign and security policy and home
affairs to intergovernmental agreements.[41] It would still be relatively
easy for states to construct coalitions to block one another's actions, yet
the Union would extend the EC's policy scope and increase its powers.

The significance of the Treaty was not that it immediately created a
politically integrated Union. It lay in the attempt by member states to

respond to the challenges of 1989 and 1990 by committing themselves to additional common goals and policies. Even though much dispute would be possible over what these policies were to be and how they were to be implemented, the principle of developing common stances in economic and monetary policy, foreign and security policy, social policy, cohesion policy and aspects of home policy implied a considerable extension and strengthening of the EC regime.

The prospects for the Union remained uncertain for a year after the rejection of the Union Treaty in the Danish referendum of June 1992. The narrowness of the outcomes in the ratification processes in France, Denmark and Britain, together with the wave of discontent over the Community in the countries which ratified the Treaty, indicated the difficulty of sustaining the integration process. Germany and other states hinted that they might be willing to go ahead with a smaller Community rather than proceed at the pace of the slowest. Meanwhile, the damaging currency turbulence before and after the French referendum in September 1992 made the prospects for achieving EMU in 1996 appear unlikely. Nevertheless, the Edinburgh Council in December 1992 gave an impressive demonstration of the member states' resolve to overcome the Community's post-Maastricht problems. Despite widespread expectations of failure, the Council reached agreement on a formula to accommodate the Danes, on financing, on provisions for subsidiarity and transparency, and on other issues.

Although it was clear that the governments of the Twelve were determined to complete the Treaty, in practice the Community appeared to be taking on a 'multi-speed' character. In monetary policy, the Treaty on European Union had explicitly permitted a degree of variability by envisaging that only the states which achieved the convergence targets would adopt a common currency, and by permitting Britain and Denmark to opt out of the third stage. In practice, too, the ERM developed into a variable-speed system, with Britain, Denmark and Greece outside the system, Germany and the Netherlands tied by narrow bands, and the other EC members remaining in the system but within wide bands. At the same time, *de facto* groupings outside the Community framework had become important – for example, the Deutschmark zone, through which Denmark, Austria and Switzerland had pegged their currencies to the Deutschmark until 1992. Finland, Norway and Sweden were also effectively in this zone until 1992 since they had pegged their currencies to the ecu.[42]

In migration policy, only nine member states (the original Six together with Greece, Portugal and Spain) became signatories to the

Schengen Agreement, since not all Community members could agree on a common policy for the movement of people and for border controls, and a number were unwilling to place this area under Community competence. The pattern was one of concentric circles. Germany and the Benelux countries formed a core group, with closely linked economies, membership of the Western European Union (WEU) and NATO, and participation in the Schengen Agreement and the ERM. France was close to this core, only standing outside NATO's integrated command. Italy was also close, but outside the ERM. Spain and Portugal were not so closely linked economically as the original six, but they were members of Schengen, the ERM, NATO and the WEU. Greece was in NATO, and had agreed to join Schengen and the WEU, but remained outside the ERM. The UK was in NATO and the WEU, but was outside the ERM and the Schengen agreement, and had opted out of the third stage of EMU and the Social Chapter. Denmark was a member of the ERM and NATO, but had only observer status at the WEU, and had opted out of EMU and was outside Schengen. In terms of the arrangements which operated in practice, therefore, west European countries were operating a variable geometry of regimes, with different membership in different policy areas.[43]

Meanwhile the EC continued to develop differentiated relationships with other European states in the north, east and south. The closest relations were with EFTA, which was brought into the extended Single Market through the agreement on the European Economic Area. Next were the Europe Agreements with the Visegrad countries, Bulgaria and Romania. These provided for a gradual phasing out of trade barriers (more slowly in sensitive products) and a phasing in of the four freedoms (though with free movement of capital and people deferred for a decision after 1997). The Association Agreements with Malta, Cyprus and Turkey provided for free trade and a customs union but not for the extension of the Single Market (though Turkey's agreement conceded the principle of eventual membership). The Trade and Cooperation Agreements, extended to Slovenia, Albania and the Baltic states, allowed for economic cooperation and an initial liberalization of trade, lifting the Community's Quantitative Restrictions for some but not all products. A new cooperation and partnership agreement was under consideration for Russia in early 1993, but Russian objections to the terms held up its signature.

Notwithstanding its internal difficulties, the EC proved a very powerful magnet for other European countries. Yet almost all the countries in the different categories of agreement with the EC were frustrated with the terms of the agreements, and sought either full membership or at least better terms. For the EFTA states, the European Economic Area offered an unsatisfactory 'half-way house', which required compliance with EC rules without participation in the making of those rules. For the Visegrad states, the Europe Agreements excluded trade in key sectors and were too unspecific about membership. The southern Europeans were frustrated by the indefinite delay which followed their applications. All sought membership as a means of obtaining the perceived benefits of the EC and in order to participate in its decision-making.

As for the EC members, their position on enlargement varied. France was reluctant to enlarge before further deepening was complete, and Spain attempted with some success to link enlargement to a better deal on the cohesion fund. However, the enlargement case had a considerable momentum. The inclusion of the EFTA states was in most respects uncontentious, since they were small, rich countries which already traded extensively with the EC and shared west European values and social structures. Austria, Finland, Norway and Sweden would add only 25 million people to the 345 million of the EC-12. The east European countries, as well as presenting different economic systems and security complications, would add much larger populations. The Visegrad states were much poorer and would add a further 64 million. Bulgaria, with 9 million, and Romania, with 23 million, were poorer still, while the 280 million people of the former Soviet republics and the 56 million of Turkey, all with low living standards, were a very unattractive proposition to the Community. In January 1993, Hans van den Broek, the EC Commissioner for External Affairs, ruled out membership for Russia and other former Soviet republics, suggesting that the Community would draw the line under the states with which it currently has Association or Europe Agreements (Poland, Hungary, the Czech and Slovak Republics, Slovenia, Bulgaria and Romania).[44] In April 1993 the Commission recommended that the EC should commit itself to membership for the Visegrad countries. The long-term proposal therefore appeared to be of a Union extending to the borders of the former Soviet Union, though not necessarily including all parts of eastern Europe.

The timescale for these potential accessions was dictated partly by the ability of the applicants to comply with the terms of the *acquis communautaire*, partly by the competing demands of the Community's other business. Even admitting the EFTA countries in time for the 1996 IGC posed a challenge for the negotiators. The timescale for the Visegrad group was likely to be more protracted.

It was clear that adding new members would require changes in the EC's decision-making system, for the balance between the institutions, and between the institutions and the states, could not be straightforwardly adapted to a large number of new states, several of which might be small. More fundamentally, the EC would have to modify its historical character as a defender of west European interests (for example in the original policy areas of the Community, steel and agriculture) if it was to become an institution capable of representing a wider European community.

Several courses were open for the European Community. It could remain a west European organization, deepening integration. France, and perhaps Spain and Italy, may prefer this option, but Germany, the UK, Denmark and the Netherlands appear to be committed to further enlargement. Another course was to extend membership to take in further members over a fairly long timescale. This was the policy which Kohl, Major, van den Broek and other policy-makers espoused. A further possibility might be for the *de facto* pattern of differential development to spread throughout the wider Europe, with different patterns of integration and cooperation in different policy areas.

East central Europe

Although the new states in east central Europe were in a dependent position after 1989 (as they had often been before), the international relationships in east central Europe were less troubled than in other parts of eastern Europe. Notwithstanding the Czech-Slovak split, Poland, Hungary and the Czech and Slovak Republics managed to sustain a regional cooperation agreement and maintained multilateral diplomacy with each other as well as their western neighbours, and they contained their problems over minorities without violence. Their relations with each other were peaceful, if not always harmonious.

The new governments in Poland, Hungary and Czechoslovakia all anticipated close political and economic relations with western Europe, as part of their return to Europe. Poland and Hungary were already trading with western partners as much as with those in the East by 1989, and Czechoslovakia was soon in a similar position. President Arpad Goncz expressed their aspirations in a speech in November 1991:

Working out good relations with our neighbours is a matter of coming to terms with our past and present, but we want especially to come to terms with our future and establish ourselves as part of a

91

common Europe. It is the western, or European standards of social, political and economic activities, not to speak of the western standards of living, that we want to see in Hungary, so we turn our eyes and our mind to the West above all.[45]

Regional cooperation was no more than a second-best to joining the EC, and it was not pursued with great enthusiasm. It was only under the threat of a return to hard-line government in the Soviet Union that Poland, Hungary and Czechoslovakia reached the Visegrad agreement, under which they agreed to cooperate in foreign affairs, security, defence, and the pursuit of European integration. There was, at first, little in the way of economic integration to buttress this cooperation: rail and road links between the states were relatively poor and there was no wish at first to deepen economic cooperation with former Comecon partners if this risked being perceived as an alternative to the EC. Several disputes made cooperation difficult: between Czechoslovakia and Poland, because of the uneven pace of reforms in the two countries;[46] between Slovakia and Hungary, because of the disputed Gabcikovo-Nagymaros dam[47] and the Hungarian minority in Slovakia; and between the Czech lands and Slovakia, over the break-up of the federation. Nevertheless, the Czech–Slovak divorce proceeded without violence, and Hungary and Slovakia agreed to submit their dispute to arbitration.

The east central European states gradually restored links with the countries to their east, especially Ukraine, which expressed interest in joining the Visegrad group and the Central European Initiative. Hungarian policy-makers urged western investment in Hungary as an efficient and cost-effective means of reaching former Soviet markets, and passing on modernization eastwards. Similarly, Poland and Slovakia were interested in exploring economic cooperation with Ukraine. They wanted their place in the system of concentric circles, between their more developed western neighbours and their poorer neighbours to the east.

For Hungarian policy-makers, the key to the future was first an open Europe, and secondly the adoption of European norms and standards. Hungary was seen to be on the western border of a line dividing Europe into an area of stable, developed, secure societies to the west and an area of instability to the south and east.[48] Hungarian policy-makers urged accelerated accession into western regimes as a means of projecting stability in the east. They saw a clear alternative between rapidly establishing a system of democratic practice and European standards, on the one hand, and risking a slide into nationalism and ethnic conflicts on the other. A western Europe that allowed entry by stages and was open to eastern societies, including the Balkans and former Soviet republics if they fulfilled European standards, would provide stability to the continent and hold open the possibility of integration.

In addition to seeking entry to the EC, Poland, Czechoslovakia and Hungary wanted early NATO membership. They agreed to press for this at the time of the Soviet coup in August 1991, and continued to seek it afterwards. This was not because they perceived any immediate military threats; it was overspill from national minority conflicts that appeared to pose the immediate security threat. Nevertheless, these states were in a security vacuum. The North Atlantic Cooperation Council (NACC) gave them a consultative status with NATO, but without any security guarantee. With regard to both NATO and the EC, they were in an antechamber. But an intermediate position between involvement in multilateral institutions and a renationalized security and foreign policy could not be sustained indefinitely.

The Balkans: return to anarchy?

If most of Europe after the Cold War became regionalized, the Balkans once more became balkanized, the states of that region once again forming a miniature international system, in which power politics held sway and war and the threat of war were immediate realities. The region became characterized by bilateral ties and a pattern of tacit alliances rather than multilateral diplomacy.

In Yugoslavia the death of Tito and the collapse of communist rule destroyed the fabric which had held the country together. The federal system, which balanced power between the large republics, slowly broke down, and the newly elected nationalist leaders in Croatia and Serbia set the course which led to war.

The Yugoslav war thus became the first great test of how the West would respond to the new conflicts in eastern Europe. It was not a test for which either the CSCE or the EC was well prepared. The CSCE, which had only just developed its dispute settlement procedures, was blocked by Yugoslavia's vetoes and therefore handed over the lead role to the EC. The EC at first attempted to hold Yugoslavia together when (with hindsight) it was no longer possible, and then under German pressure recognized Croatia before it was necessary to do so and before the EC Arbitration Commissioner's conditions for minority rights had been met. EC monitors were relatively ineffective, and the Community's mediation attempts suffered from confusion with its power-broking role. After the fighting began in Bosnia, the EC was obliged to hand the lead to the UN, the only body with real expertise and experience in managing this type of conflict. The crisis found the members of the EC sharply divided. The British argument for non-intervention signalled a profound reflex to avoid military engagement as well as a traditional 'realist' view that intervention was neither in the British interest nor likely to be effective. Germany's decision to recognize Croatia, which forced the EC's hand, indicated an assertive use of the EC for obtaining its own policy preferences, together with an inclination to support a traditional friend.

In the midst of the crisis, the mainly Muslim Bosnian government demonstrated a remarkable sense of European standards and upheld a vision of a civic, non-ethnically based Bosnia–Herzegovina. Its leaders wished to maintain cultural heterogeneity, to respect the different religious traditions, and to oppose exclusive policies. 'We have no minorities', insisted Dr Silajdzic, the Foreign Minister.[49] But as the siege of Sarajevo got under way, it was sadly clear that such values had no weight in the new Balkan environment. Crude force of arms was the only source of power.

As the conflict threatened to engulf Kosovo and Macedonia, a pattern of bilateral diplomacy began to develop in the Balkans, in which fears about minorities and historical suspicions again played important roles. Greece supported Serbia and blocked the EC's recognition of Macedonia for many months; Albania sought peaceful unification with the Albanian communities in Kosovo and Western Macedonia; Bulgaria recognized the Macedonian state but not the Macedonian nation. The fear of the war spreading was an important factor in the region, but despite the strength of nationalism and the fragmentation of the international system, there were also important signs of restraint: in Kosovo, for example, where the ethnic Albanians for long pursued a policy of non-violent resistance, and in Sofia, where the government declared that it would not involve itself in regional axes or alliances and that it would avoid intervening in the war even if it spread, and called on other states in the region to do the same.

Unlike in the early twentieth century, major states outside the region were reluctant to intervene on a unilateral basis (though the United States and Russia supported different sides verbally). The United States and west European countries worked through international organizations, especially the UN, to arrange humanitarian relief and the peace conferences under Lord Carrington, Lord Owen and Cyrus Vance, and to seek to prevent the conflict spreading by pre-emptive stationing of admittedly very limited observer and peacekeeping forces. The neighbours of former Yugoslavia also avoided direct involvement, and Bulgaria, Romania and Greece maintained their westward orientation, although the growing tensions in the region and fears that the war might spread affected them all. Despite the efforts of the UN and non-governmental organizations, the war continued to rage; in the absence of western enthusiasm for what seemed likely to be a long and costly intervention, or of sufficiently powerful and well-supported domestic opposition to the war in the former Yugoslav republics, the new European order was shown to have little capacity to enforce its norms against local warlords. It seemed that a security community with extensive international institutions in one part of Europe could coexist with war-fighting in another. Yet the effects of the war in Yugoslavia were deeply damaging to aspirations for a wider Europe based on CSCE norms. The west European states had first ignored the condition of minority protection in their recognition of Croatia; next, they came close to endorsing frontiers changed by force in the proposals for a settlement put forward at the Geneva Peace Conference. In terms of political symbolism, the war and the European response to it were coming to define the character of the post-Cold War order.

Russia and the CIS

The former Soviet Union was another large area in which fragmentation of political power and the absence of effective multilateral institutions laid a basis for disorder and potential conflict. At a time when Russia was further removed from western and central Europe than at almost any time in its history, Russian foreign policy was inclined to look south and east, and above all to the 'near abroad' of the neighbouring republics.[50] The question of how Russia and the other republics would fit into the new European international system remained unclear while turbulent political developments clouded the prospects for economic and political reform.

The Russian attitude to western Europe and specifically to the EC had begun to change from suspicion to cooperation during the 1980s, as part of Gorbachev's foreign policy reappraisal. Gorbachev's notion of the Common European Home emphasized his desire to establish a European identity for the Soviet Union. In the late 1980s the Soviet Union established diplomatic relations with the EC, and in December 1989 a trade and cooperation agreement was signed. The decision to let eastern

Europe go (or rather, to avoid military intervention to sustain the Soviet bloc) reflected a further fundamental change. From 1990 to 1991 criticism of these policies gained strength in the conservative reaction which led to the August coup, but the defeat of the coup and the transfer of power to Yeltsin confirmed the pro-western and pro-west European orientation of the new government.

The break-up of the Union, however, created a new state system, and it was to be some time before a new pattern of foreign relationships would crystallize. Eleven of the fifteen former Soviet republics agreed to form the Commonwealth of Independent States in December 1991, but only Russia and the four central Asian republics participated fully. Ukraine, in particular, resisted attempts to create CIS institutions and its establishment of national armed forces undermined the objective of military integration. Mainly as a lever for bargaining purposes, Ukraine, Belarus and Kazakhstan refused to hand their nuclear weapons over to Russia. In practice relations between the new states developed on a bilateral basis and the CIS became chiefly a framework for intergovernmental and defence cooperation between Russia and the other member states. Even this role withered away when Russia abolished the CIS joint military command in June 1993.

With weak central control, the foreign policies of the new states began to drift apart. Relations between Ukraine and Russia became tense, as disputes developed over the Crimea, the Black Sea Fleet and economic policy. In 1992–3 these disputes were settled or deferred, but strains remained. In July 1993 the Russian parliament alarmed the Ukranians by claiming that Sevastopol was Russian territory, though President Yeltsin repudiated the claim. Ukraine established good relations with Hungary and signed agreements with Poland and other east European states, although its application to join the Visegrad group did not proceed. Ukraine also sought membership of the EC. Russia, too, expressed interest in joining the EC, NATO and the Council of Europe, but no positive responses were forthcoming. Russian relations with the United States and the West remained important, especially since financial aid was essential to underpin economic reform, although successive lurches in policy jeopardized the large sums that were promised. Meanwhile Russian relations with central and eastern Europe took a lower priority than those with neighbouring states. Cut off by other states from central Europe, and with the central Asian republics as its most reliable neighbours, Russia increased the emphasis on its Eurasian and national interests in its foreign policy-making.

Within the Russian Federation, the weakness of the centre left much of the power in the hands of regional power centres, and within the former Soviet Union security problems and violent conflicts were multiplying as the breakdown of the old order led national groups and new states to press claims to territory and economic assets. The position of the Russian minorities outside Russia caused considerable concern. Other republics viewed Russian efforts to secure stability and mount peace-keeping operations in the former Soviet Union with great suspicion and were nervous of the re-emergence of a post-imperial role. They also feared a harsher and more interventionist policy if nationalist forces came to power in Moscow. In 1992–3, however, despite these trends towards fragmentation, Russian foreign policy remained relatively re-strained and Russia was still willing to use the CSCE and other multilateral frameworks as a forum for discussing the conflicts in the former Soviet Union.

The response of the West and western Europe was conditioned by an awareness of the stakes involved in the developments in the former Soviet Union, but also by a sober caution about large-scale investment in an economy subject to high inflation, collapsing output and a large state industrial sector which was resistant to reform. Western advisers and institutions became deeply involved with the radical reform programme devised by Yegor Gaidar. Offers of help even increased after his fall from power when Yeltsin's future seemed threatened by the constitutional crisis, but in practice the scale of assistance, when set against the magnitude of the crisis, was limited. Nevertheless multi-level economic, political and institutional engagement in the problems of the transition remained the best available course for the West. There was a very good case for sustaining support for democratization, demilitarization and economic recovery.

The Baltic states

The Baltics were a special region by virtue of their history as independent democracies in the interwar period. Their return to statehood, confirmed in 1991 by the collapse of the Soviet Union, which they had precipitated, raised once again the issue of how these small states could maintain their independence next to a larger and much more powerful Russia. Tensions developed between the Baltic governments and the Russian minorities, especially in Estonia and Latvia. To these were added the disputes over the continued presence of Russian troops in all three Baltic states, over border controls, unauthorized overflights by Russia, the transit of oil, and territorial issues. The Estonian situation was the most serious, and the new citizenship law of 1993, which required the Russian minority to pass a language test if they were to continue to reside in Estonia, alarmed Russian-speakers and the Russian government.

The Baltic states sought cooperative links with the other western states bordering the Baltic, as well as with the EC and the US. Understandably, the West was cautious about making commitments to these societies while Russian troops remained in place. The Baltics, with the support of the Nordic states, sought to move out of the periphery of Russia into the periphery of the EC and the Nordic countries, but it has not been easy for them to avoid being influenced by events in their large neighbour.

Conclusion: security in the new Europe

The new security risks were therefore primarily those of fragmentation and nationalist conflicts, in place of conflict between blocs. This presented a fresh challenge to the security institutions which had been adapted to Cold War conditions.

NATO had been a powerful institution in the Cold War period, and it remained one of the main multilateral institutions through which the United States exercised influence in Europe. But in the absence of immediate threats, it was difficult for NATO to sustain its role. The strength of Atlanticism was declining in Germany, and Americans were becoming less willing to shoulder a large part of the defence burden for the Europeans. Pressure from the French and German governments for a European defence structure split European states into those (Britain, Denmark and the Netherlands) which wished to retain NATO as the main vehicle of collective defence and those (France, Germany and Italy) which wished to develop a European defence identity. The compromise in the Treaty on European Union was to upgrade the WEU as a European pillar of the Alliance, with the proviso that this would not affect existing Alliance commitments.

While the choice between a European and an Atlantic defence identity remained unresolved, the pressing issue was whether and how to enlarge the western collective defence system. The east central Europeans wanted to join; so did Russia. NATO was concerned that if its security system advanced eastwards Russia would feel threatened; moreover there was little enthusiasm to become embroiled in the conflicts on the edges of this region.[51] Instead, NATO set up NACC as a forum for all the members of the former Warsaw Pact. The WEU extended its membership by inviting accession by the remaining members of the European Union, and associate membership for the remaining European members of NATO; in November 1992 it took in Greece as a full member and Turkey and Norway as associates. Denmark and Ireland were willing only to be observers. The Treaty on European Union permits new members of the Union to be eligible for WEU membership, so in principle this is an alternative route for states to enter the western collective defence system. In the immediate aftermath of the Cold War, however, there was no western intention to extend a security guarantee to east European societies.

Sweden, Norway and Austria were in a different position. Their traditional policies of neutrality began to change in response to the new environment. This was, in part, forced by the EC, which insisted that new members would have to accept the *finalité politique*, including the possibility of an ultimate defence identity. In June 1991, Sweden's then Prime Minister, Ingvar Carlsson, said in a statement to the Riksdag, 'Sweden's security policy is based on a firm and consistent policy of neutrality ... We would not be obliged to participate in a possible future defence alliance between EC states or in possible collective security arrangements. If in the future, a durable European security order is established, based for example on the CSCE, the foundations on which Sweden's policy of neutrality has rested hitherto will change.'[52] The following year Prime Minister Carl Bildt said, 'Now we are living in a different Europe. We can no longer refer to our foreign and security policy as a policy of neutrality, and although we have no plans to join any military alliance, we see our future active participation in the efforts to shape a common foreign and security policy as a crucial contribution to the security of the whole of Europe.'[53]

The end of the Cold War had brought the end of the bloc confrontation and led to realignments in security organizations. The major structural change was the disintegration of the eastern bloc, which returned eastern Europe to a fragmented system based on national security planning. The West retained its collective security system, though it too was altered by the changing relationship between the United States and the European allies and the emergence of the WEU as the European pillar of the alliance. The CSCE survived as a cooperative security framework, and a security regime persisted in the shape of the CFE and other arms control agreements; but the renationalization of security policies in eastern Europe complicated the task of these structures. Earlier proposals to turn the CSCE into a collective security system had little chance of acceptance; indeed, the trend was away from unifying security organizations.

The main security risks in the immediate post-Cold War period arose from conflicts within states, especially ethnic and national conflicts, and their potential overspill into interstate conflicts. While traditional military forces developed a new role as peacekeeping and intervention forces, the Council of Europe and the CSCE developed another kind of response, oriented towards preventing conflicts by seeking political solutions within affected countries. The CSCE High Commissioner on National Minorities, for example, was given the task by CSCE member states of communicating between governments and national minorities, in potentially dangerous situations which had not yet erupted into violence.[54] The Council of Europe similarly began to develop community-building measures between different national groups. These transnational responses offered a new approach to security problems.

Besides these 'fire-fighting' measures, however, a longer-term policy is plainly needed. The basis of security in western Europe and the OECD has been the existence of a 'security community', which makes fighting incredible among its members. The development of such a security community cannot be achieved by security policy alone, but depends on a broader consensus of values and the spread of institutions for managing and regulating conflict. The strong evidence for the finding that democracies do not fight other democracies suggests that extending democratization is one element of establishing a security community. Measures to mitigate economic insecurity and to assist dialogue between communities and cultures are others.

One of the results of the end of the Cold War has been the wide acceptance of a broader meaning of security. For example, ministers of WEU member states declared at their Petersberg meeting in June 1992 that 'security in its broadest sense encompasses not only military but also political aspects, respect for human rights and fundamental freedoms, as well as economic, social and environmental aspects'.[55] The challenge for those concerned with the European order is to find ways to enhance security in this sense by developing measures that will influence areas of eastern Europe which are in a state of fragmentation. Assistance with economic transformation and democratization are important here, since economic insecurity and weak institutions for domestic conflict resolution are primary sources of disorder.

Jacques Delors, in a speech discussing the management of interdependence among EC members, identified four features that he regarded as critical. The first was exchanges and cooperation between peoples. The second was the control of economic interdependence, through competition, cooperation and cohesion. The third was the framework of law and common rules. The fourth was an effective decision-making process.[56]

If these principles are applied as a test against which the management of interdependence in the wider Europe can be judged, it is evident that the emerging relationships were strongly asymmetric. The end of the Cold War did free the movement of peoples, but because of weak currencies and adverse rates of exchange in eastern Europe, most of the movement was one-way. Control of economic interdependence was largely in the hands of west European states. Integration of law and rules was on the basis of western models. East European societies had only limited access to the decision-making processes which governed these transactions.

Extending membership of west European institutions to east European states is only a partial response to this asymmetry: a fuller one requires both greater dialogue between societies and the adaptation of institutions to societies in a spirit of partnership.

6

EUROPE AND THE WORLD: CONCLUSIONS

External influences on the European order

The preceding chapters have examined some of the European trends which are shaping the new European order. Wider international developments will also have their influence. Some of these have been discussed: the influence of globalization, the trends towards a more closely integrated world economy and regional economic integration, and the shift from a bipolar to a core–periphery world order. A number of other exogenous trends which are likely to influence the European order can be identified, although a full discussion of them is not possible here.

The disintegration of one superpower and the relative decline of the other have brought to an end a period when the political influence of European states was reduced and constrained. In principle the re-emergence of Europe after the Cold War allows Europeans once again the choice to shape, or to fragment, the order of their continent. However, the partnership with the USA continues to be vital to western Europe, in economic, political and security terms, and US involvement in the provision of aid, investment and finance to Russia and eastern Europe is critical in the central and east European transition. The maintenance of the partnership depends on domestic political factors in the United States as much as in Europe. The emphasis on domestic interests in the election which brought President Clinton to power suggests the possibilities of strains in the relationship. As the management of western interests moves from US leadership to a partnership of large industrial powers, policy-making may be less clear-cut and more subject to confusion and disagreement. In the short term, the influence of the West, following the collapse of communism, is riding high. In the longer term, however, the cohesion and primacy of the American–European partnership cannot be assured.

The end of the Cold War led to regionalization not only in Europe but also in other areas of the world. Central Asia, for example, re-emerged from the period of Soviet domination with renewed assertion of national and cultural identities, but a power vacuum developed which attracted commercial, political and religious penetration by neighbouring regional powers. The complex politics of the region indicate the new importance of powers such as Turkey and Iran.

The collapse of the bipolar system has brought into prominence the arc of instability that surrounds Europe, ranging from North Africa, through the Middle East, to Central Asia and the peripheral areas around Russia. Many of these areas have weak economies and rapidly rising populations. For example, the population of North Africa is expected to be equal to that of Europe by 2000. Migration into Europe is increasing rapidly and conflicts in neighbouring regions are likely to generate not only political problems for European states and their partners, but also additional flows of people.

To some extent this arc of instability coincides with the Christian–Muslim divide, which became more salient after the Cold War. The history of conflict between the two civilizations persists and mutual understanding remains poor, although differences between states within each of these culture-areas overlay the cultural divide. This cultural element has combined with core–periphery tensions to generate anti-western reactions, in the form of radical fundamentalism (as in Iran) or radical secular nationalism (as in Iraq), and, conversely, anti-Muslim reactions in Europe.

The way in which European societies respond to these challenges in some respects parallels their response to eastern Europe; there is the same choice between defensive and engaging policies. The EC's developing network of external policies includes trade agreements with the North African states, and the CSCE's efforts to develop a cooperative security structure in the Mediterranean indicate a readiness to extend an open Europe; but the increasingly restrictive response to migration from the south suggests elements of Fortress Europe. The interdependence of societies in these and other issue-areas is not confined to Europe but spreads to adjacent regions. More broadly, the global issues of climate change, deforestation and resource use link European decisions with those of the rest of the world. The balance between seeking to manage these issues through international institutions and regimes and furthering short-term national or regional interests is one which will have great

103

political implications in shaping the wider post-Cold War order.

The external impact of European change

No less important are the ways in which change in Europe influences the rest of the world. A fragmented Europe is likely to be associated with a growth in nationalism and fragmentation in other parts of the world and a weakening of global institutions and regimes. A Fortress Europe will tend to induce competitive attempts to establish regional economic and political integration; it would be likely to be associated with the strengthening of trade blocs and sharper conflict both within the core and between the core and the periphery of the world system. A wider Europe would tend to be linked to more extensive building of international institutions and transnational contacts with other parts of the world.

The Single Market has already had a powerful international impact, both on the formation of similar systems of regional economic cooperation in North America and East Asia, and on patterns of trade and investment. Economic forecasters suggested that the Single Market would contribute to growth among the EC's trade partners, especially in areas (such as East Asia) which have a comparative advantage in labour costs to offset the European comparative advantage in capital-intensive sectors.[1] This effect will only be felt when the EC emerges from recession. If the current recession is followed by trade diversion towards the EC and a drift into protectionism, the mutual effects will be negative. The Single Market may have a much less beneficial effect on developing countries, which are increasingly marginalized in an extremely competitive, high-technology world economy. It is difficult for them to break out of their role as primary producers, trading raw materials on unfavourable terms.[2]

The Union Treaty, when and if it is finally ratified, may also be expected to have an international impact, insofar as the member states succeed in consolidating a common foreign policy and monetary system and, especially, if they move eventually towards a common defence. In principle the EC can deploy a considerable battery of policy instruments, but the mixed record of coordination of foreign policy to date, together with the difficulty of coordinating monetary, trade and foreign policies, have cast doubt on whether the Community is capable of becoming a powerful actor on the world stage in any area other than commercial policy.

The west European states retained separate areas of interest and special relationships outside Europe. Britain still kept the vestiges of the special relationship with the USA and of its links with Commonwealth countries. France maintained close relationships with North and Central Africa. Spain still had close ties with Latin America. Italy played a special role in the Mediterranean. There were also separate interests inside Europe; for example, Germany and Greece had conflicting Balkan allegiances, and there were latent differences of interest between France and Germany in east central Europe. In principle the European Union might unify these separate interests and relationships into a whole, but this is a very long-term prospect.[3]

What seems significant and novel about the Community as a new political system is that it has led to a unique system of power-sharing and transnational integration in a region of dense population and diverse national and cultural traditions. Amongst its many other legacies to the world, Europe is responsible for the spread of its state system (and of its form of nationalism) to the rest of the world. Changes in this system in Europe may represent a new evolutionary line in the world history of nations and states. If the European Union were to develop simply into another large state or to break down as a basis for cooperation, this experiment would come to an end; but if it is capable of sustaining and developing a community of diverse societies, the significance of this will not be limited to Europe.

Conclusions

The European order is in a period of transition from the Cold War, and a settled new order has yet to crystallize. Its future development is subject to four major uncertainties: the future of west European integration, the stability of unified Germany, the outcome of the transformation of east central Europe, and the political future of Russia and the CIS.

Nevertheless it is possible to identify the inadequacies of existing paradigms. The view of Europe as an anarchic system of states is difficult to sustain given the progress of west European integration. The old paradigm of west European integration also cannot be sustained without modification. The model of integration as it worked in the past was particularly adapted to western Europe and rested on the gradual development of a *modus vivendi* between west European states and between the states and EC institutions. But the challenge of enlargement and of German unification makes it difficult to continue along the traditional path of progressive extensions in functional integration. The Franco-

German relationship, which was the basis of the original Community, no longer seems capable of playing the central role in the enlarged Community that is in view. In the former communist societies of eastern and central Europe, the changes of 1989–91 have dramatically overturned the order that was established for 45 years, and the emergent order is a distinctive blend of elements from the traditional past and the unfamiliar present. The new paradigms of international regimes and transnational societal transactions are becoming important, but they do not yet apply across the whole of the wider Europe. The European international order is a complex hybrid of the new and the old, the multi-level society and the newly established nation-state.

Despite the uncertainties, some conclusions can be established. The development of a single integrated European market is a process with powerful dynamic consequences, which has affected most of the peripheral parts of Europe. The relationships between state, society and international institutions are showing signs of change throughout Europe, and the nation-state is under strain from the opposite pulls of globalization and nationalism. In western Europe, the nation-states adapted to the difficulty of managing economies which have outgrown national borders by pooling elements of their sovereignty. However, integration is developing unevenly, and a pattern of 'concentric circles' has developed, with some states pooling powers in more issue-areas than others. Taken in conjunction with the graduated system of agreements with European states outside the Community, the whole of Europe up to the boundaries of the former Soviet Union can be seen as a core–periphery structure. Some of the newly independent republics may also take a place in this structure, but Russia, because of its size, its resources and its political traditions, seems likely to remain a separate political and economic centre, which will retain its gravitational pull on nearby states. At least some of the Visegrad countries, Bulgaria and other east central European states seem likely to succeed in their economic transformation and to become candidates for inclusion in an enlarged European Community, or more immediately in an increasing number of the circles of cooperation and integration which are developing around it. The development of a wider Community also appears to be an interest of a majority of the member states, and especially of Germany, although the present trends suggest that this might take on a more hegemonic character than the applicant states would desire. The member states which fear a loss of influence or of economic position in an expanded Community may resist enlargement for some time, but a wider Europe currently seems the most plausible of the scenarios.

This conclusion is subject to a number of qualifications and conditions. If the process of disintegration in the former Soviet Union becomes very violent, the military-security issue-area could again become dominant, and west Europeans may then prefer a defensive Fortress Europe, based on a Union with stronger military cooperation, to a looser, wider Europe. If economic recession is deep and prolonged, sustaining any degree of economic and political integration may become difficult, and if future crises (perhaps in eastern Europe) threaten the compatibility of interests of existing member states, then a return to a fragmented Europe is conceivable. The process of market development and the political development of eastern Europe are also critical; if east European economies fail to pull out of their slump and fall into authoritarianism, then the wider Europe scenario would be impossible to sustain.

Much can be done to strengthen the basis for a wider European community of societies. Stronger all-European institutions and common frameworks of norms are desirable in order to mitigate the fragmentation inherent in an anarchical nation-state system. They should be supplemented by cross-national contacts between societies at the level of citizens, local governments and regions. In order to sustain both its diversity and a degree of stability, Europe needs to move beyond the constraints of the state system to develop a well-interconnected, multi-level international society.

For the immediate future, the relationship between the EC and east European states will be based on the Europe Agreements, which provide a broad framework for political cooperation. These can be strengthened, to improve market access, especially in the sensitive sectors, and to build on the provisions for political dialogue. The European Political Area that the Commission has proposed could be developed strongly as a basis for participation in common policies. In principle the three-pillar structure of the Union allows for extension of intergovernmental cooperation in foreign and security policy and over home and justice affairs. The Commission has proposed enlarged meetings of the European Council with ministers from central and east European states. In order to strengthen participation in institutions at other levels, states with Europe Agreements might be invited to elect parliamentarians to participate as observers and later as representatives in the European Parliament.

Much can also be done to foster economic development of the central and east European societies. Indeed, assisting economic development, demilitarization and democratization is an essential part of a broadly conceived policy aimed at averting the security implications of the failure of political and economic transition.

All the states of the region are already members of the CSCE, and in April 1993 the Council of Europe included the Visegrad group and Bulgaria. Strengthening these organizations would therefore consolidate cooperation in the wider Europe. For example, the useful CSCE post of Commissioner on National Minorities could be developed and the work of the Council of Europe in support of democratization and the protection of minorities is a basis for strengthening domestic capacities to resolve and manage conflict.

Despite its many flaws, the European Community is the strongest European institution to survive the Cold War, and the one with the strongest claim to become the foundation upon which a wider community of European societies might be organized. It will have to adapt and transform itself if it is to move from being a west European body to an organization capable of meeting the diverse needs and aspirations of people and societies throughout the wider Europe. However, if it can form the basis for a wider and durable pluralistic security community, this would be a response worthy of the European challenge.

NOTES

Chapter 1: Past European orders

1 Hugh Seton-Watson, *Eastern Europe 1918–41*, London: Cambridge University Press, 1944, p. 68.
2 F.H. Hinsley, *Power and the Pursuit of Peace*, Cambridge: Cambridge University Press, 1979.
3 Hans G. Schenk, *The Aftermath of the Napoleonic Wars*, London: Kegan Paul, 1947; quoted in Kaveli J. Holsti, *Peace and War: Armed Conflicts and International Order 1648–1989*, Cambridge: Cambridge University Press, 1991.
4 Sidney Pollard, *European Economic Integration, 1815–1970*, London: Thames and Hudson, 1974.
5 Quoted in Hinsley, *Power and the Pursuit of Peace*.
6 From 1880 to 1914, German arms expenditure rose by a factor of five; British and Russian by a factor of three; and French by a factor of two. A.J.P. Taylor, *The Struggle for Mastery in Europe, 1848–1918*, Oxford: Clarendon Press, 1954.
7 Quoted in Joe Scott, *The World Since 1914*, Oxford: Heinemann, 1989.
8 See Judy Batt, *East Central Europe from Reform to Transformation*, London: RIIA/Pinter, 1991.

Chapter 2: Paradigms and paradoxes

1 This view of scientific advance was popularized in Thomas Kuhn, *The Structure of Scientific Revolutions*, Chicago: University of Chicago Press, 1970. Kuhn's influential concept of paradigms is itself, of course, a paradigm.
2 Hedley Bull, *The Anarchical Society: A Study of Order in World Politics*, London: Macmillan, 1977.

3 Robert Keohane and Joseph Nye, *Power and Interdependence*, London: Harper Collins, 2nd edn, 1989, p. 25.

4 Stephen Krasner, 'Structural Causes and Regime Consequences: Regimes as Intervening Variables', in Krasner (ed.), *International Regimes*, Ithaca, NY: Cornell University Press, 1983.

5 K. Waltz, *Theory of International Politics*, Reading, MA: Addison-Wesley, 1979.

6 R. Keohane, *After Hegemony: Co-operation and Discord in the World Political Economy*, Princeton, NJ: Princeton University Press, 1984.

7 Peter van Ham, *The EC, Eastern Europe and European Unity: Discord, Collaboration and Integration since 1947*, London: Pinter, 1993, Chapter 11.

8 Karl W. Deutsch et al., *Political Community and the North Atlantic Area: International Organization in the Light of Historical Experience*, Princeton, NJ: Princeton University Press, 1957.

9 Ernst B. Haas and Philippe C. Schmitter, *The Politics of Economics in Latin America: The Latin American Free Trade Association after Four Years of Operation*, Denver, CO: Social Science Foundation and Graduate School of International Studies, University of Denver, 1966.

10 Joseph S. Nye, Jr, *Peace in Parts: Integration and Conflict in Regional Organization*, Boston: Little, Brown, 1971.

11 Paul Taylor, presentation at Chatham House, 12 November 1992.

12 Anna Michalski and Helen Wallace, *The European Community: The Challenge of Enlargement*, London: RIIA, 2nd edn, 1992.

13 Deutsch, *Political Community and the North Atlantic Area*.

14 Keohane and Nye, *Power and Interdependence*.

Chapter 3: Towards a European economic space?

1 See Margaret Sharp, 'Tides of Change: The World Economy and Europe in the 1990s', *International Affairs*, vol. 68, no. 1, January 1992.

2 GATT, *International Trade, 1990–91*. See also Peter Dicken, 'European Industry and Global Competition', in David Pinder (ed.), *Western Europe: Challenges and Change*, London: Belhaven Press, 1990.

3 Anna Murphy, *The European Community and the International Trading System*, vol. 1, Centre for European Policy Studies, Brussels, Paper No. 43, 1990, pp. 10–15.

4 Gerrit Zalm and André de Yong, 'Long-Term Scenarios of the World Economy', *OECD Forum for the Future*, Paris: OECD, 1991, p. 3; Dicken, 'European Industry and Global Competition', p. 41.

5 Soogil Young, *OECD Forum for the Future*, Paris: OECD, 1991.

6 Stephen Thomsen and Stephen Woolcock, *Direct Investment and European Integration: Competition among Firms and Governments*, London:

RIIA/Pinter, 1993.

7 Wolfram Hanrieder, *Germany, America, Europe*, New Haven, CT: Yale University Press, 1989.

8 Michael Smith and Stephen Woolcock, *The United States and the European Community in a Transformed World*, London: RIIA/Pinter, 1993.

9 Per Magnus Wijkman, 'Patterns of Production and Trade', in William Wallace (ed.), *The Dynamics of European Integration*, London: RIIA/Pinter, 1990.

10 Thomsen and Woolcock, *Direct Investment and European Integration*.

11 Dicken, 'European Industry and Global Competition'.

12 Thomsen and Woolcock, *Direct Investment and European Integration*.

13 Keohane and Hoffman argue that EC decision-making since 1985 has to be explained in terms of forces in the world political economy, 'spillover', and intergovernmental bargains; see their chapter on 'Institutional Change in Europe in the 1980s', in R. Keohane and S. Hoffman (eds), *The New European Community: Decision-making and Institutional Change*, Boulder, CO: Westview, 1991.

14 *European Economy*, No. 7, July 1992, Supplement A.

15 Loukas Tsoukalis, *The New European Economy: The Politics and Economics of Integration*, Oxford: Oxford University Press, 1991.

16 Ibid; Table 8.1.

17 Ibid.

18 Stephen Padgett, 'The New German Economy', in Gordon Smith et al. (eds), *Developments in German Politics*, London: Macmillan, 1992.

19 Chris Flockton, 'The Federal Republic of Germany', in David Dyker (ed.), *The National Economies of Europe*, London: Longman, 1992.

20 Elke Speidel-Walz, *German Economic Bulletin, June 1992*, Morgan Grenfell Economics, London.

21 *Guardian*, 6 February 1993.

22 See Padgett, 'The New Germany Economy'.

23 For detailed case-studies, see David Dyker on the Soviet Union, Mark Schaffer on Poland and Paul Hare on Hungary in Dyker (ed.), *The National Economies of Europe*.

24 David Dyker, 'Soviet Union', in Dyker (ed.), *The National Economies of Europe*.

25 S. Zagashvily, 'Russian Internal versus External Integration', *Oxford International Journal*, Summer 1992.

26 A.K. Kozminski, 'Transition from Planned to Market Economy in Hungary and Poland', *Studies in Comparative Communism*, vol. 25, no. 4, December 1992, pp. 315–33.

27 Wolfgang H. Reinicke, *Building a New Europe: The Challenge of Systems Transformation and Systemic Reform*, Washington, DC: The Brookings Institution, 1992, Table A-6.

28 Ben Slay, 'East European Economies', RFE/RL *Research Report*, vol. 2, no. 1, 1 January 1993.

29 Mark Schaffer, 'Poland', in Dyker (ed.), *The National Economies of Europe*.

30 Kozminski, 'Transition from Planned to Market Economy in Hungary and Poland'.

31 Slay, 'East European Economies'.

32 Judy Batt, *Czechoslovakia in Transition: From Federation to Separation*, Discussion Paper No. 46, London: RIIA, 1993.

33 Malinka Kaparanova, 'The Bulgarian Economy in Transition: Macroeconomic Policy and Performance 1991–2', paper given at a Round Table in Chatham House, 3 March 1993.

34 J.M.C. Rollo and J. Stern, *Growth and Trade Prospects for Central and Eastern Europe*, National Economic Research Associates, Working Paper No. 1, May 1992.

35 S.M. Collins and D. Rodrick, 'Eastern Europe and the Soviet Union in the World Economy', *International Economics*, No. 32, Washington, DC: Institute for International Economics, 1991.

Chapter 4: Nation, state, union

1 Gordon Smith, *Politics in Western Europe*, Aldershot: Dartmouth, 1990.

2 Frederico Romero, 'Cross-border Population Movements', in William Wallace (ed.), *The Dynamics of European Integration*, London: RIIA/Pinter, 1990.

3 *Eurobarometer*, No. 35, June 1991.

4 A people may be dispersed, such as the Jews outside Israel and British expatriates. A nation links a sense of territoriality, citizenship, and political culture. Anthony D. Smith, *The Ethnic Origins of Nations*, Oxford: Blackwell, 1986.

5 Ibid.

6 Anthony D. Smith, *National Identity*, London/Harmondsworth: Penguin, 1991.

7 Hugh Seton-Watson, *Nations and States*, London: Methuen, 1977.

8 James Mayall, *Nationalism and International Society*, Cambridge: Cambridge University Press, 1990.

9 The Austrian government, for example, concluded that the only way Austria could have real sovereignty in an interdependent world was by joining the EC. Anna Michalski and Helen Wallace, *The European Community: The Challenge of Enlargement*, London: RIIA, 1992.

10 This argument is developed in Mary Kaldor, *Notes on European Institutions, Nation-States and Nationalism*, Science Policy Research Unit, University of Sussex.

11 William Wallace, 'The Changing Role of the State in Western Europe', paper for RIIA/ESRC Seminar, 15 March 1991.

12 Albert Bressand, 'The Pan-European Integration Watershed', in *Europe in Search of a Map*, Paris: Project Prométhée Perspectives, 1992, p. 44.

13 For a detailed discussion of these trends, see L.J. Sharpe, *The Rise of Meso Government in Europe*, London: Sage, 1993.

14 Interview with Dr Demes, Slovak Ministry of International Relations.

15 Wolfgang Wessels, 'Administrative Interaction', in Wallace (ed.), *The Dynamics of European Integration*.

16 Seymour M. Lipset and Stein Rokkan, 'Cleavage Structures, Party Systems and Voter Alignments: An Introduction', in Lipset and Rokkan (eds), *Party Systems and Voter Alignments: Cross-National Perspectives*, New York: Free Press, 1967; quoted in Jan-Erik Lane and Svante O. Ersson, *Politics and Society in Western Europe*, London: Sage, 1991.

17 Lane and Ersson, *Politics and Society in Western Europe*, pp. 175–92.

18 Charles Powell, presentation at RIIA Study Group on 'Changing Trends in Governance in the Wider Europe', 6 May 1992.

19 John Ardagh, *Germany and the Germans*, London/Harmondsworth: Penguin, 1991.

20 Peter Merkl, *A New German Identity* (quoting Emnid-Informationen), in Gordon Smith et al. (eds), *Developments in German Politics*, London: Macmillan, 1992, p. 336.

21 Russell J. Dalton, 'Two German Electorates?', in Smith et al. (eds), *Developments in German Politics*, p. 74.

22 Roland Sturm, 'Government at the Centre', in Smith et al. (eds), *Developments in German Politics*.

23 Roland Sturm, 'The Changing Territorial Balance', in Smith et al. (eds), *Developments in German Politics*.

24 Günter Grass, *Two States, One Nation? The Case Against German Unification*, London: Secker and Warburg, 1990.

25 George Schöpflin, 'The Political Traditions of Eastern Europe', in Stephen R. Graubard (ed.), *Eastern Europe ... Central Europe ... Europe*, Boulder, CO: Westview, 1991.

26 Ibid.

27 John Hiden and Patrick Salmon, *The Baltic States and Europe: Estonia, Latvia and Lithuania in the Twentieth Century*, London: Longman, 1991, pp. 46–8 and pp. 56–8.

28 Richard Crampton, *A Short History of Modern Bulgaria*, Cambridge: Cambridge University Press, 1987.

29 Information from Ivo Indjev, Director General, Bulgarian Telegraph Agency.

30 For a full account, see Judy Batt, *East Central Europe from Reform to Transformation*, London: RIIA/Pinter, 1991.

31 Alexander Likhotal, formerly of the International Affairs department of the Central Committee of the CPSU, is the source for this date.

32 Interview with Pal Tamas, 31 March 1992.

33 Interview with Pal Tamas, 31 March 1992. Hungarians refer to the 'uncle-nephew' relationship, in which people return favours or loyalty for acts of patronage.

34 Rudolf Andorka, 'Hungary: Counting the Social Cost of Change', *The World Today*, vol. 49, no. 4, April 1993.

35 Judith Pataki, 'Hungary: Domestic Political Stalemate', *RFE/RL Research Report*, vol. 2, no. 1, 1 January 1993, pp. 92–5.

36 Commission of the European Communities, *Central and Eastern Eurobarometer: Eighteen Countries Survey – Autumn 1992*, no. 3, February 1993.

37 Hanna Suchocka, Prime Minister of Poland, speech at Royal Institute of International Affairs, 3 March 1993.

38 Heinrich Vogel, 'Transformation in the East: The Gurus and the Mantras', *The World Today*, vol. 49, no. 4, April 1993.

39 Jan B. de Weydenthal, 'Controversy in Poland over "Euroregions"', *RFE/RL Research Report*, vol. 2, no. 16, 16 April 1993, pp. 6–9.

40 Schöpflin, 'The Political Traditions of Eastern Europe'.

41 Gellner offers a case for four time zones: western Europe, the former Holy Roman Empire, eastern Europe, and Russia. He suggests that the development of nationalism followed five stages, from the national sovereign states of the Congress of Vienna, to the nationalist irredentism of 1870–1914, to nationalism's triumph and defeat in the world wars, the genocidal phase of the Second World War, and the modification of nationalism by a multinational advanced industrial society. He also argues that the progress of nationalism varied across the four regions. Ernest Gellner, 'Nationalism Reconsidered and E.H. Carr', *Review of International Studies*, October 1992.

42 Dan Smith, *Nationalism and Security*, Briefing Paper, Amsterdam: Transnational Institute, May 1992.

43 Seton-Watson, *Nations and States*.

Chapter 5: From Cold War to hot conflicts

1 For two perspectives on the role of core and periphery in the post-Cold War order, see Barry Buzan, 'New Patterns of Global Security in the Twenty-First Century', *International Affairs*, vol. 67, no. 3, 1991, pp. 431–51; and Kinhide Mushakoji, 'Political and Cultural Background of Conflicts and Global Governance', in Kumar Rupesinghe and Michiko Kuroda, *Early Warning and Governance*, London: Macmillan, 1992.

2 In the case of steel, for example, the entry into the world market of 50

million tonnes of steel from central and eastern Europe, and the potential entry of 160 million tonnes from Russia, was a matter of concern to west European steel-makers; EC production of 130 million tonnes was already in recession. 'A giant is drawing near our doorstep', said Ruprecht Vondran, president of the German Steel Industry Association. 'We must be prepared to give it its due place while keeping it from demolishing our house.' *Europe*, no. 5960, 15 April 1993.

3 Council of Europe, *People on the Move: New Migration Flows in Europe*, Strasbourg: Council of Europe Press, 1992.

4 Sarah Collinson, *Europe and International Migration*, London: RIIA/ Pinter, 1993.

5 Patricia Chilton, 'Social Movements, Transnational Coalitions and the Transformation Processes in Eastern Europe', in Thomas Risse-Kappen, *Bringing Transnational Relations Back In: Non-State Actors, Domestic Structures and International Institutions*, University of Wyoming, forthcoming. See also Owen Greene, 'Transnational Processes and European Security', in Michael C. Pugh (ed.), *European Security – Towards 2000*, Manchester: Manchester University Press, 1992.

6 Richard von Weizsäcker, 3 October 1990, in *Deutsche Aussenpolitik 1990/ 1: Auf dem Weg zu einer europäischen Friedensordnung*, Bonn: Auswärtiges Amt, 1991.

7 Conference on Security and Cooperation in Europe, *Charter of Paris for a New Europe*, Paris: CSCE, 21 November 1990.

8 Ibid.

9 Kalevi J. Holsti, *Peace and War: Armed Conflicts and International Order 1648–1989*, Cambridge: Cambridge University Press, 1991, pp. 340–3.

10 For an elaboration of these points, see Oliver Ramsbotham and Hugh Miall, *Beyond Deterrence: Britain, Germany and the New European Security Debate*, London: Macmillan, 1991.

11 Hans-Günter Brauch, *Institutional Components of a European Security Architecture*, paper presented to the Pan-European Conference of the European Consortium for Political Research, Heidelberg, September 1992, p. 12.

12 International Institute for Strategic Studies, *The Military Balance*, London, 1992.

13 Conference on Security and Cooperation in Europe, *The Challenge of Change*, Helsinki, 1992; Rachel Brett, *The Development of the Human Dimension Mechanism of the CSCE*, Human Rights Centre, University of Essex, 1992.

14 Horst Teltschik, 'Vom "politischen Zwerg" zur "Weltmacht" – Nachdenken über Deutschlands neue Rolle in Europa', in *Die Welt*, 22 September 1990; quoted in Renata Fritsch-Bournazel, *Europe and German Unification*, Oxford: Berg, 1992.

15 Eckart Arnold, 'German Foreign Policy and Unification', *International Affairs*, vol. 67, no. 3, 1991, pp. 453–71.

16 Hans-Dietrich Genscher, 'Kontinuität und Wandel', in Genscher (ed.), *Nach vorn gedacht*, Bonn aktuell, 1987, p. 19; quoted in Lothar Gutjahr, *Beyond the Trade-state: Germany's Search for a New Foreign and Defence Policy*, Mimeo, October 1992.

17 Hans-Dietrich Genscher, quoted in Brigid Laffan, *Integration and Co-operation in Europe*, London: Routledge, 1992, p. 184.

18 *Frankfurter Allgemeine Zeitung*, 18 May 1991, quoted in Gutjahr, *Beyond the Trade-state*.

19 Alfred Dregger, speech to the American Institute for Contemporary German Studies, Johns Hopkins University, 5 May 1988; quoted in Gutjahr, *Beyond the Trade-state*.

20 Helmut Kohl, speech at the Kommandeurstagung in Würzburg, 13 December 1988, *Bulletin der Bundesregierung*, No. 175/1988, p. 1550, quoted in Gutjahr, *Beyond the Trade-state*.

21 Quoted in Barbara Lippert, 'The History of the Unification Process', in Barbara Lippert and Rosalind Stevens-Ströhmann, *German Unification and European Integration*, London: RIIA/Pinter, 1993.

22 David Spence, *Enlargement without Accession: The EC's Response to German Unification*, Discussion Paper No. 36, London: RIIA, 1992.

23 Lippert, 'The History of the Unification Process'.

24 European Parliament resolution, 24 October 1990.

25 Hans-Dietrich Genscher, 'We want a European Germany, not a German Europe', quoted in Fritsch-Bournazel, *Europe and German Unification*.

26 Gisela Hendriks, *Germany and European Integration*, New York/Oxford: Berg, 1991.

27 Wolfram F. Handrieder, *Germany, America and Europe: Forty Years of German Foreign Policy*, New Haven/London: Yale University Press, 1989.

28 Teltschik, 'Vom "politischen Zwerg" zur "Weltmacht"'.

29 A Wickert Institute poll in September 1992 showed that 84% of Germans wanted a referendum on Maastricht. A poll published in *Stern* on 23 September 1992 showed that only one in three voters would support Maastricht, and that three-quarters opposed giving up the Deutschmark. In the post-Maastricht debate, the majority of Germans favoured neither political integration nor a return to independent national policy-making outside the EC, but consolidating the status quo. A poll by the Konrad-Adenauer-Stiftung on the 'Future Role of Germany in Europe' showed that between June 1991 and January 1992 support for 'advancing political union and forgoing national independence' had dropped from 46% to 36%, support for an independent national policy was only 16% (previously 17%); the number who favoured keeping the EC as it was increased from 36% to 46%. Forschungsinstitut der Konrad-Adenauer-Stiftung, Archive

Nos 9101, 9102, 9201, quoted in Emil Kirchner, 'Controlling or Accommodating Germany', paper presented to the pan-European Conference, Heidelberg, 1992.

30 'Fight nationalism with swift unity, Kohl tells Europe', *International Herald Tribune*, 8 June 1992.

31 Ibid.

32 Brigid Laffan, *The Treaty of Maastricht: A Quantum Leap Forward or SEA Mark II?*, paper presented to the Pan-European Conference of the European Consortium for Political Research, Heidelberg, 1992.

33 *Keesings Record of World Events*, London: Longman, April 1990.

34 Mike Smith, Helen Wallace and Stephen Woolcock, 'Implications of the Treaty on European Union', in US House of Representatives, Subcommittee on International Economic Policy and Trade and Subcommittee on Europe and the Middle East of the Committee on Foreign Affairs, *Europe and the United States, Competition and Co-operation in the 1990s*, 1992.

35 *Keesings Record of World Events*, April 1990.

36 Ronald Tiersky, 'France in the New Europe', *Foreign Affairs*, vol. 71, no. 2, Spring 1992, pp. 131–46.

37 Christopher Coker 'Britain and the New World Order: the Special Relationship in the 1990s', *International Affairs*, vol. 68, no. 3, July 1992.

38 Ulla Holm, *The French Discourse on Maastricht*, paper presented to the Pan-European Conference, Heidelberg, 1992.

39 Tiersky, 'France in the New Europe', p. 139.

40 Laffan, *The Treaty of Maastricht*, p. 15.

41 *Treaty on European Union*, Luxembourg: Office of the Official Publications of the EC, 1992.

42 'Europe's Hard Core', *The Economist*, 21 November 1992.

43 Sarah Collinson, Hugh Miall and Anna Michalski, *A Wider European Union? Integration and Cooperation in the New Europe*, Discussion Paper No. 48, London: RIIA, 1993.

44 *The Times*, 29 January 1993.

45 Arpad Goncz, 'A Changing Hungary in a Changing Europe', speech to the Royal Institute of International Affairs, 20 November 1991.

46 See Libor Roucek, *After the Bloc: The New International Relations in Eastern Europe*, Discussion Paper No. 40, London: RIIA, 1992.

47 For an account from both sides, see 'Treading Water: The Danube Dam Dispute', in *East European Reporter* (Budapest), vol. 5, no. 5, October 1992.

48 Source in Hungarian Foreign Ministry, March 1992.

49 Dr Silajdzic, 'The Case for a Unified Bosnia-Herzegovina', speech to the Royal Institute of International Affairs, March 1992.

50 Sergei Karaganov, *Russia: The New Foreign Policy and Security Agenda*, Centre for Defence Studies, King's College, London, Paper 12, 1992.

51 Trevor Taylor, *NATO and Central Europe: Problems and Opportunities in a New Relationship*, Discussion Paper No. 39, London: RIIA, 1992.
52 Swedish Ministry for Foreign Affairs, *Sweden, the EC and Security Policy Developments in Europe*, Stockholm, 1991.
53 Carl Bildt, 'Europe: The Priorities for the Next Ten Years', speech to the UK Presidency Conference, London, 7 September 1992.
54 CSCE, *The Challenge of Change*, Helsinki, 1992.
55 WEU Ministerial Council, 'Petersberg Declaration', 19 June 1992, in *Europe*, no. 1787, 23 June 1992.
56 Jacques Delors, 'The European Community and the New World Order', speech to the UK Presidency Conference, London, 7 September 1992.

Chapter 6: Europe and the world

1 Kym Anderson, 'Europe 1992 and the Western Pacific Economies', *Economic Journal*, vol. 101, November 1991, pp. 1538–52.
2 Sheila Page, 'Europe 1992: Views of the Developing Countries', *Economic Journal*, vol. 101, November 1991, pp. 1553–66.
3 Curt Gasteyger, 'Europe and the Changing World Order', in Werner Weidenfeld and Josef Janning (eds), *Global Responsibilities: Europe in Tomorrow's World*, Gütersloh: Bertelsmann Foundation, 1991.

New title

European Identity and the Search for Legitimacy

edited by Soledad García

European identity is a complex notion, and one that has achieved high prominence as a result of the unification process. Are social fragmentation and cultural heterogeneity a hindrance to European unity? What does the concept mean now to the citizens of Eastern Europe, so suddenly deprived of their identity as communists? The authors, recognized experts in the field, shed light on these crucial questions of identity, legitimacy and citizenship. They examine the considerable differences between cultural traditions on the one hand and economic and political influences on the other, as well as stressing the trends towards convergence.

Contents

Publication: October 1993
by Pinter for the RIIA